Instruction

We start with a large point in the middle which we then outline with small points.

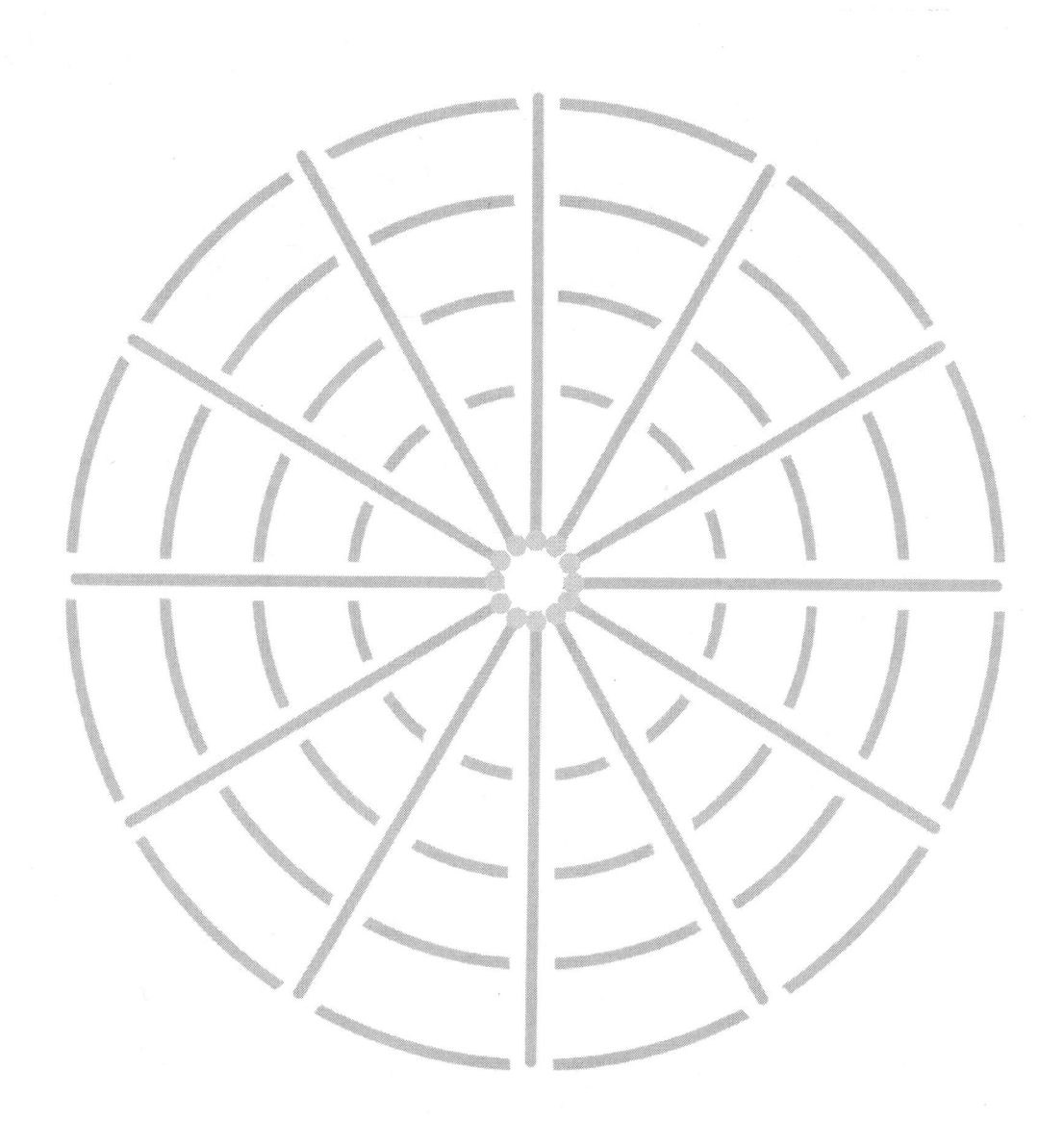

Paint the next points staggered and always get a little bigger, starting with the lightest color.

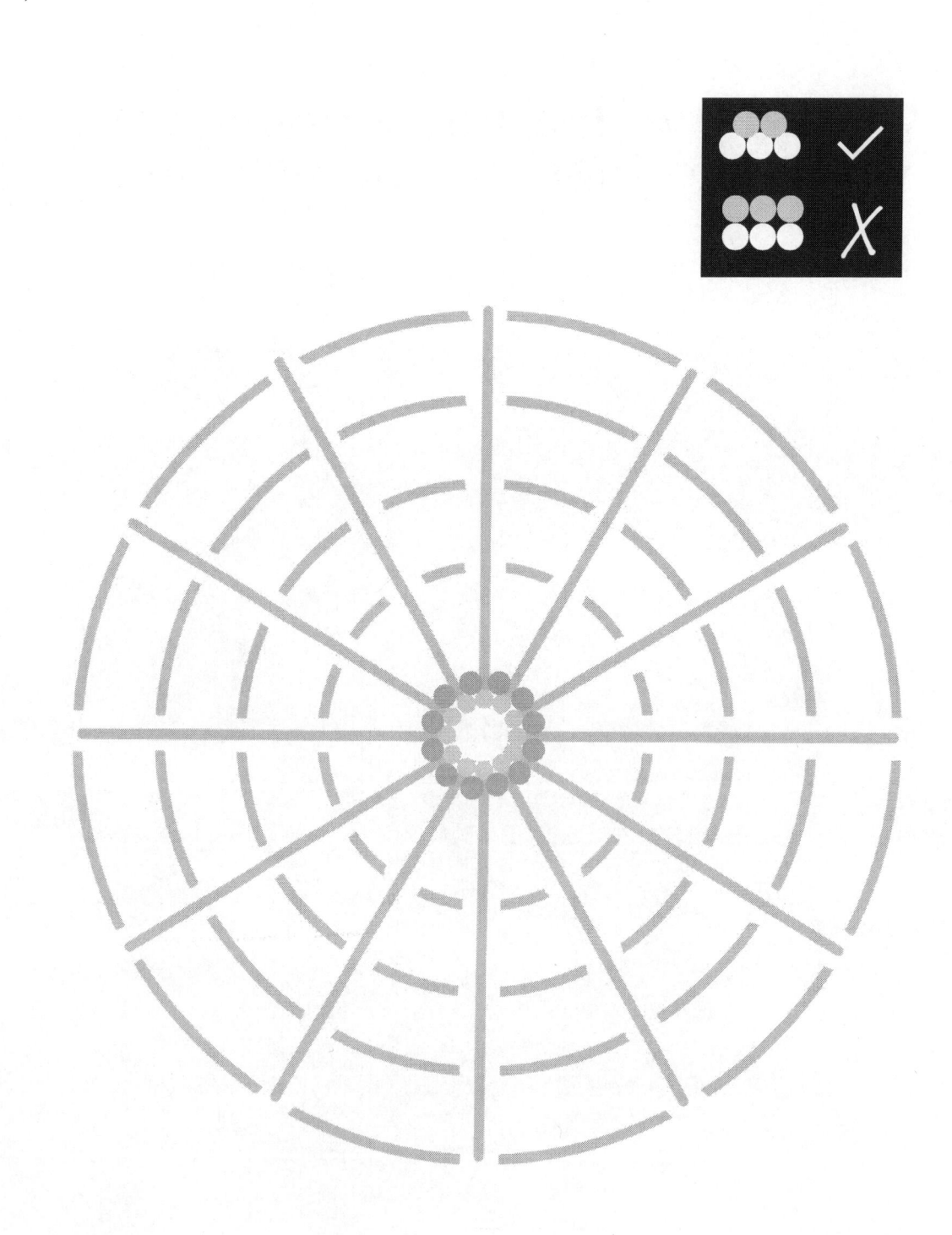

Fill the whole area with dots and get darker and darker with the color.

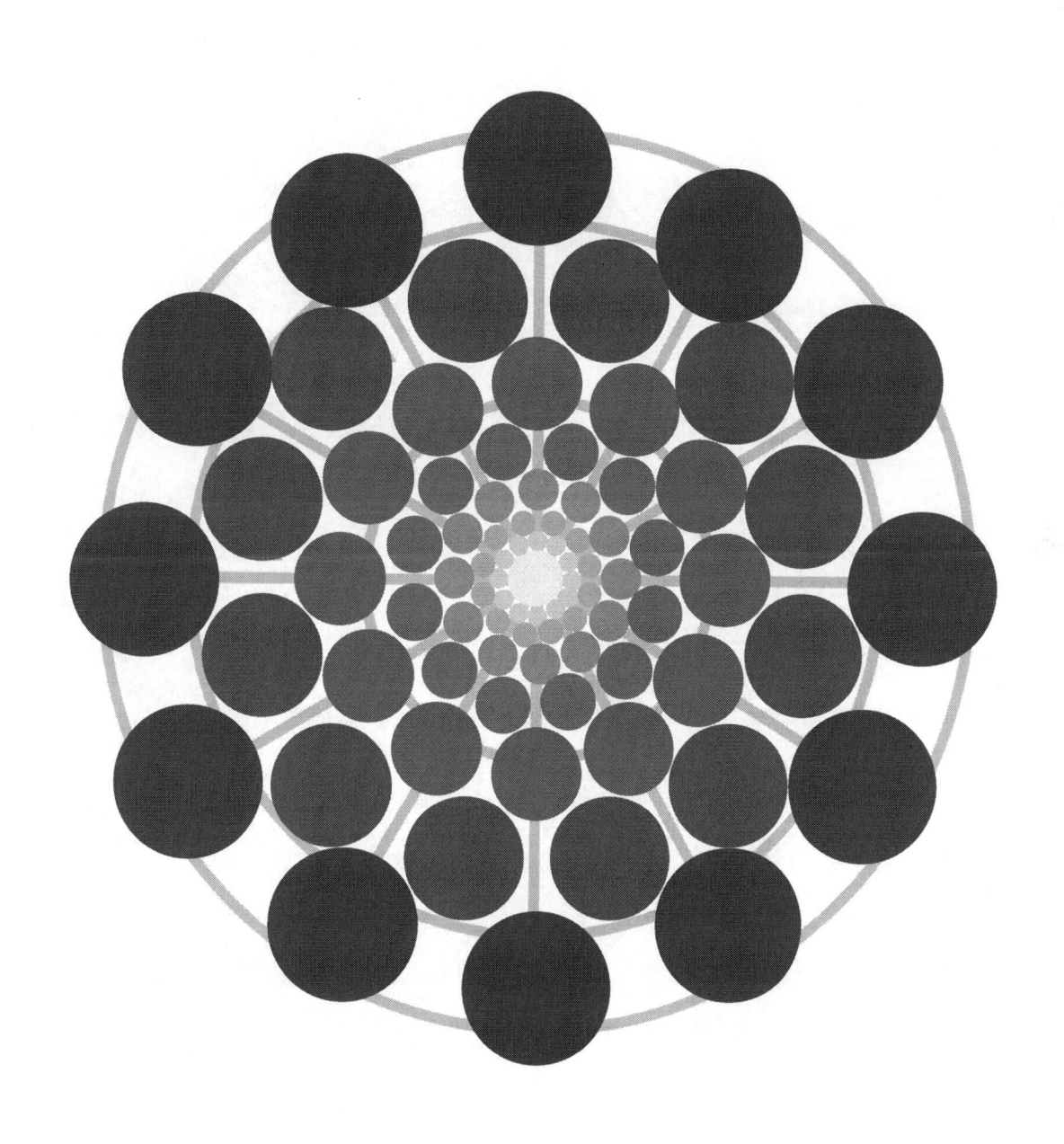

Small dots in the spaces.

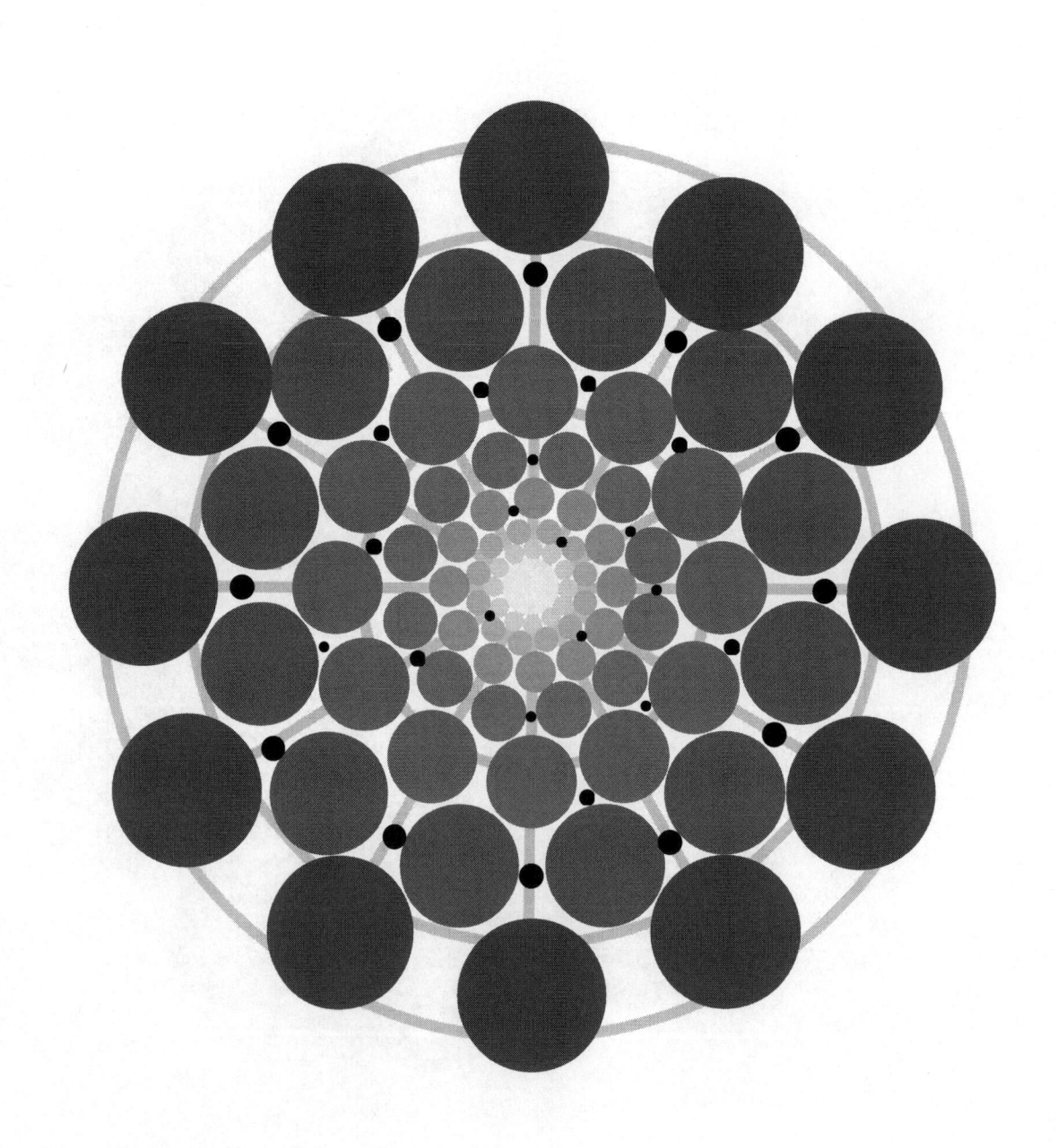

Points to points with the color of the previous row.

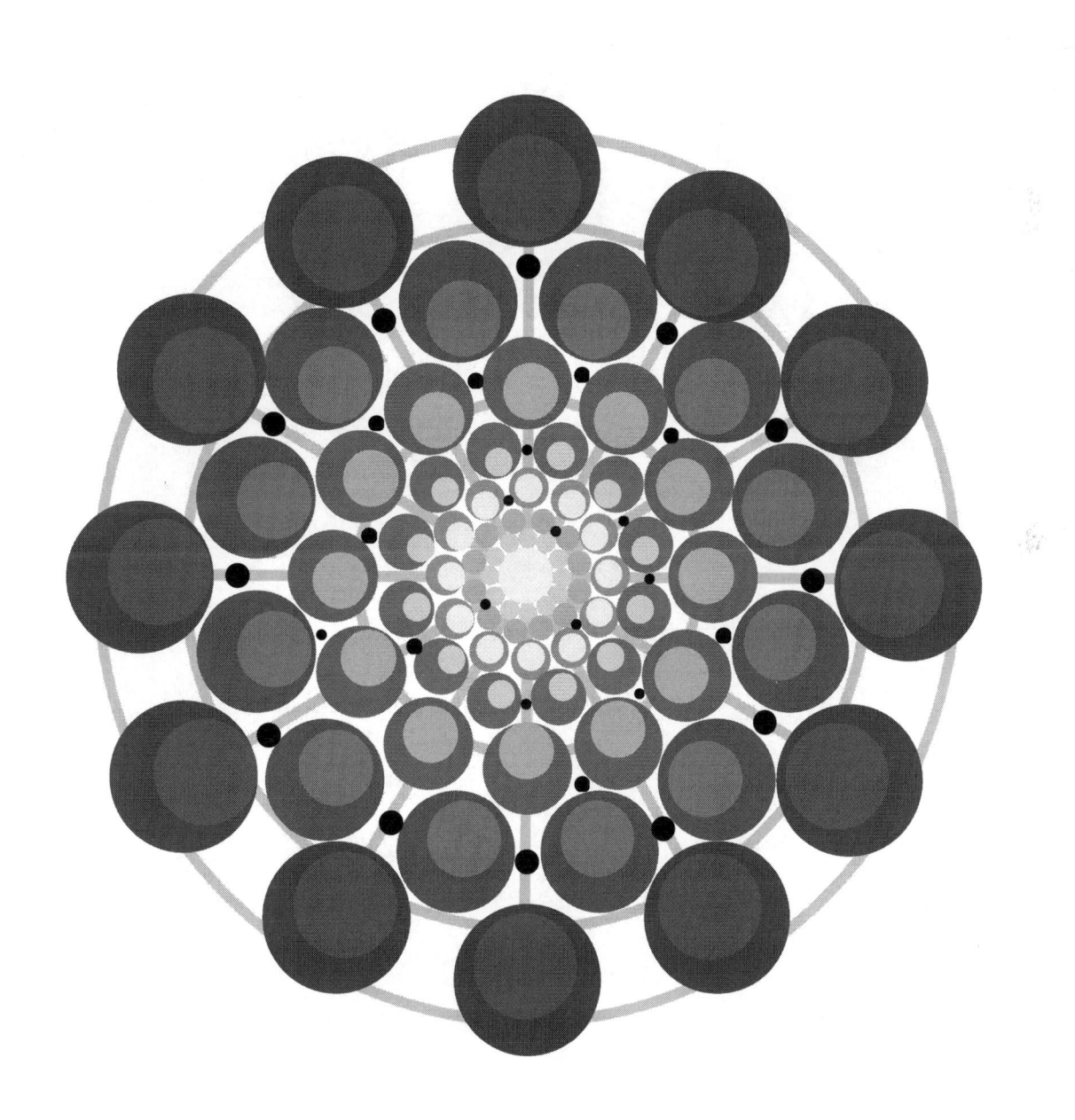

A few more points for decoration and your dot mandala is ready. :)

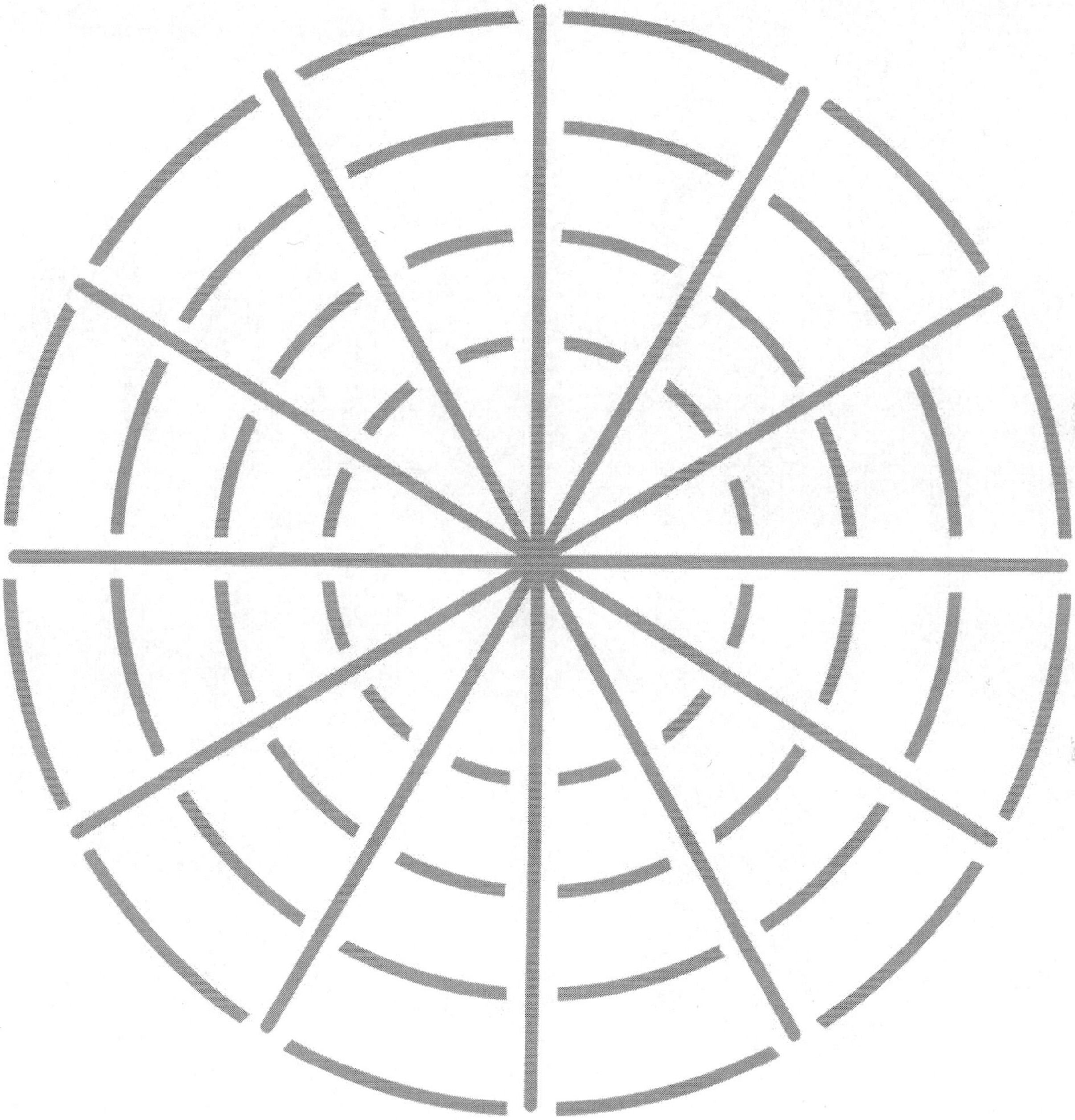

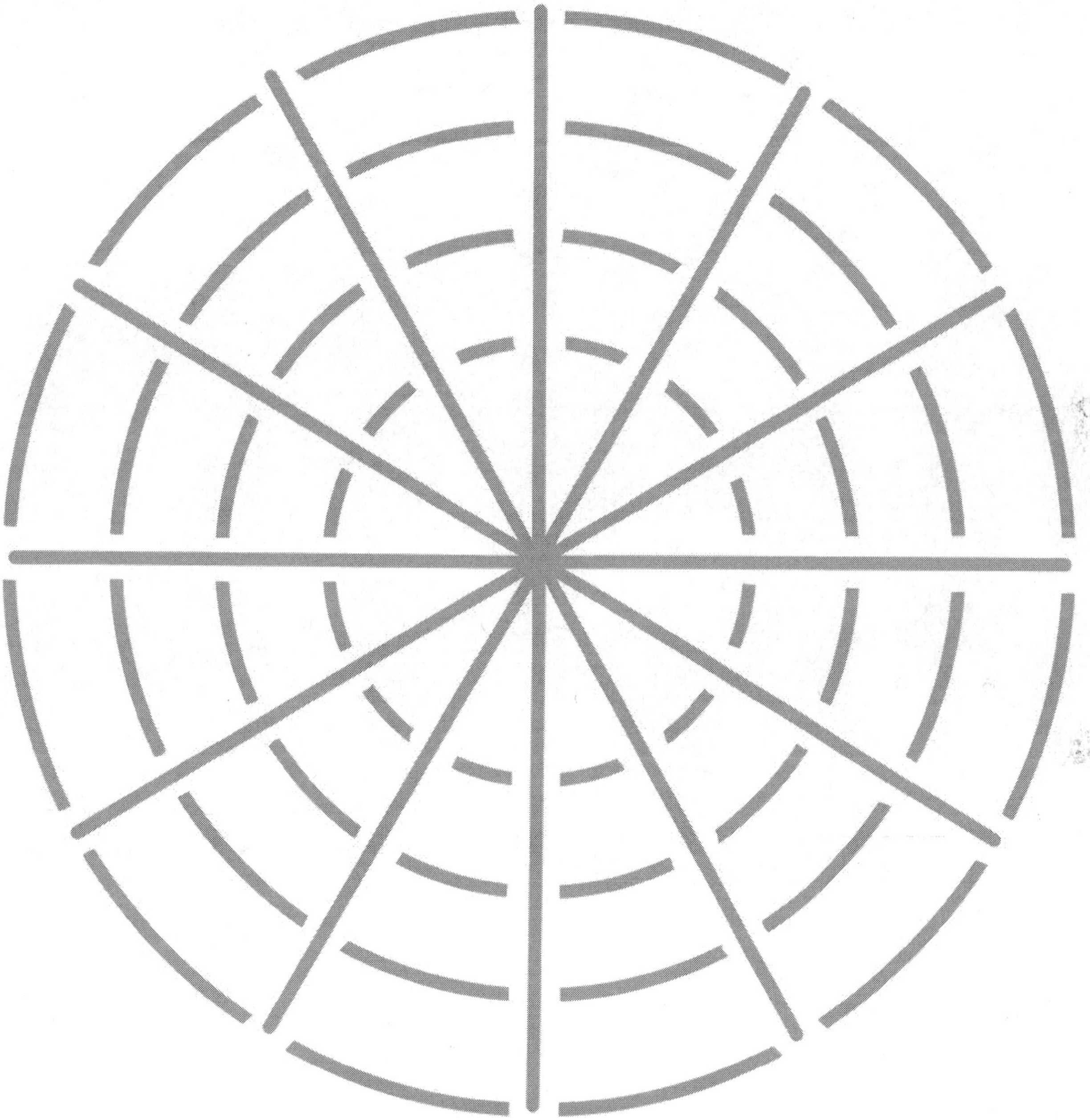

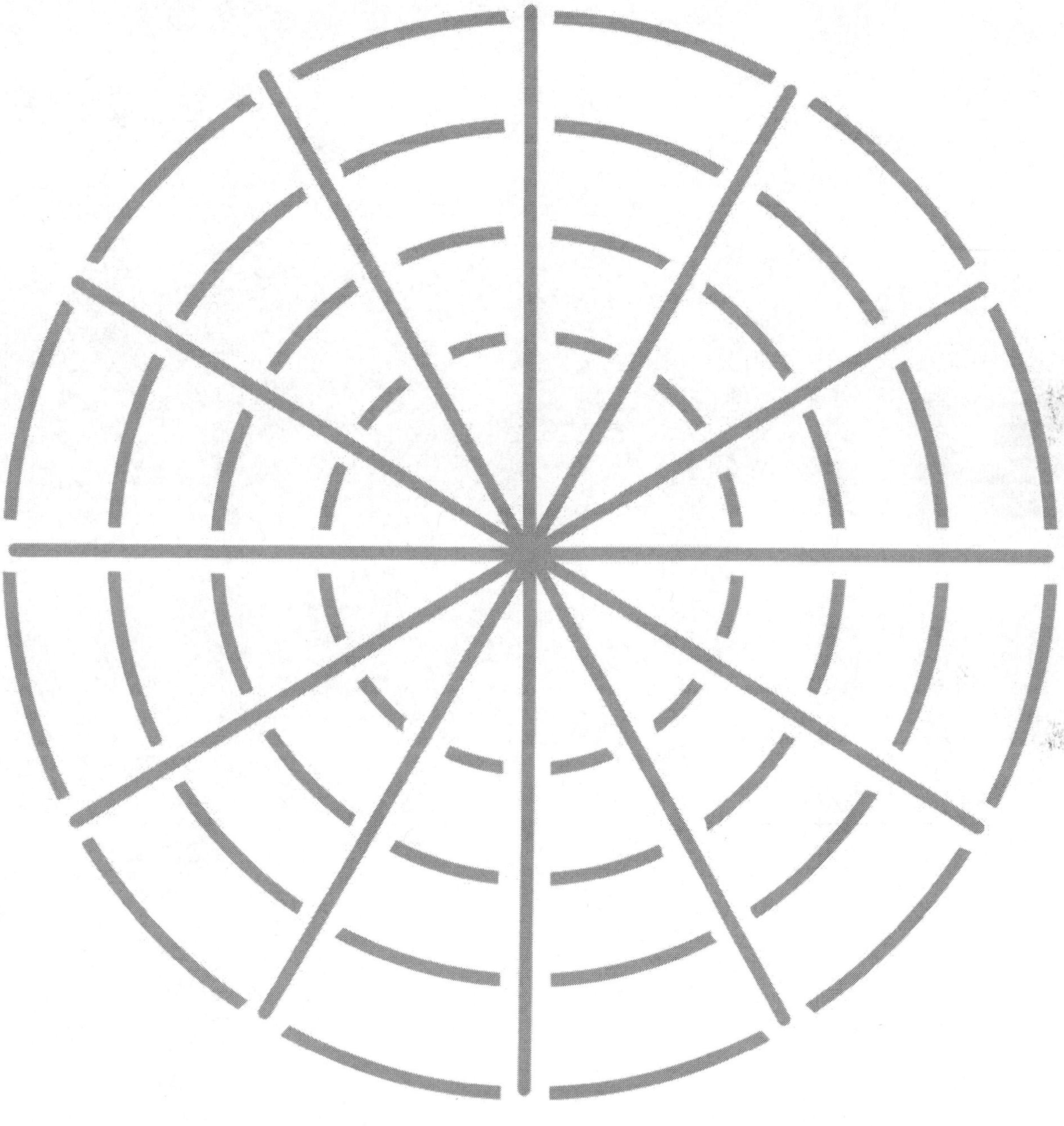

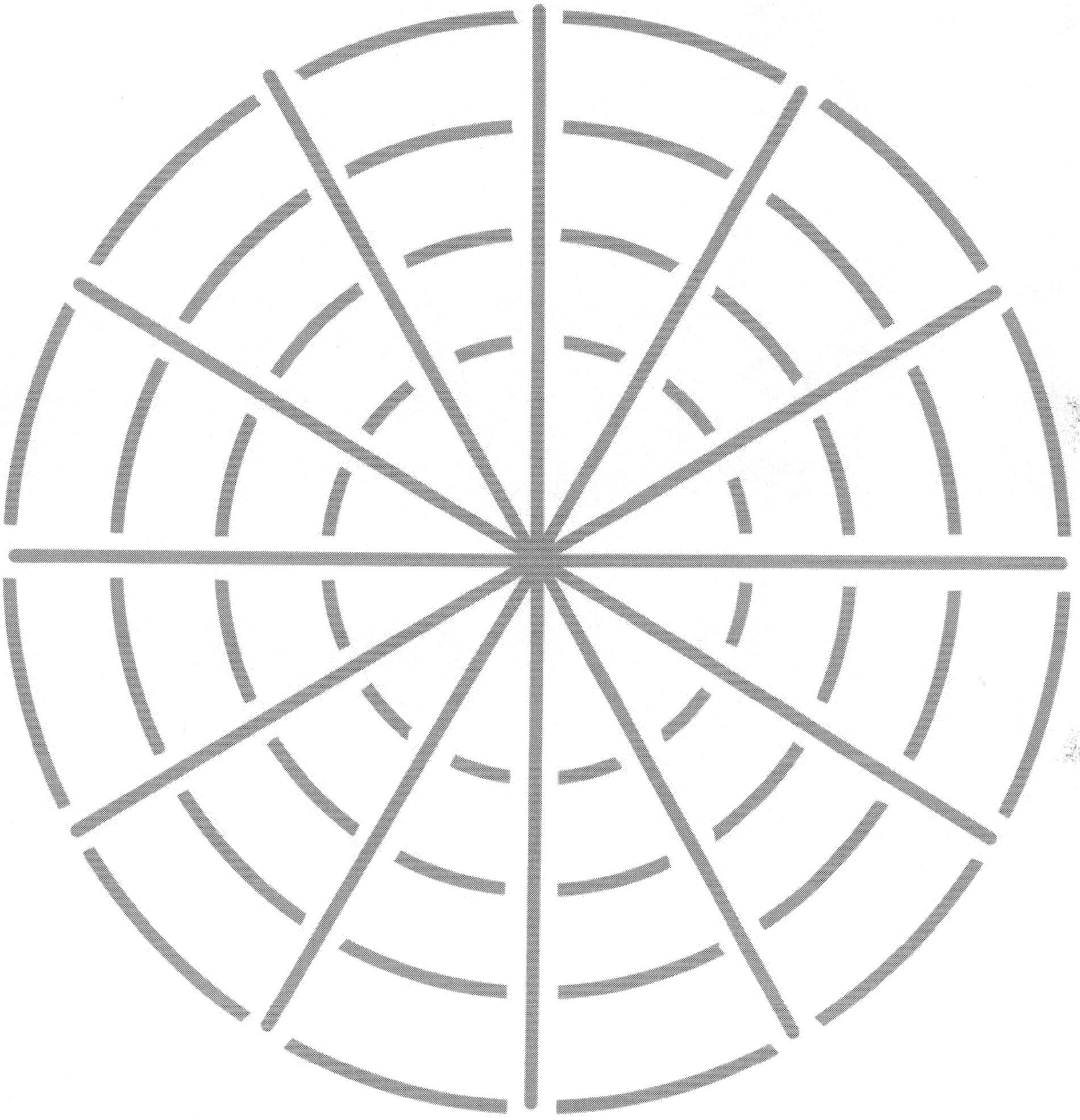

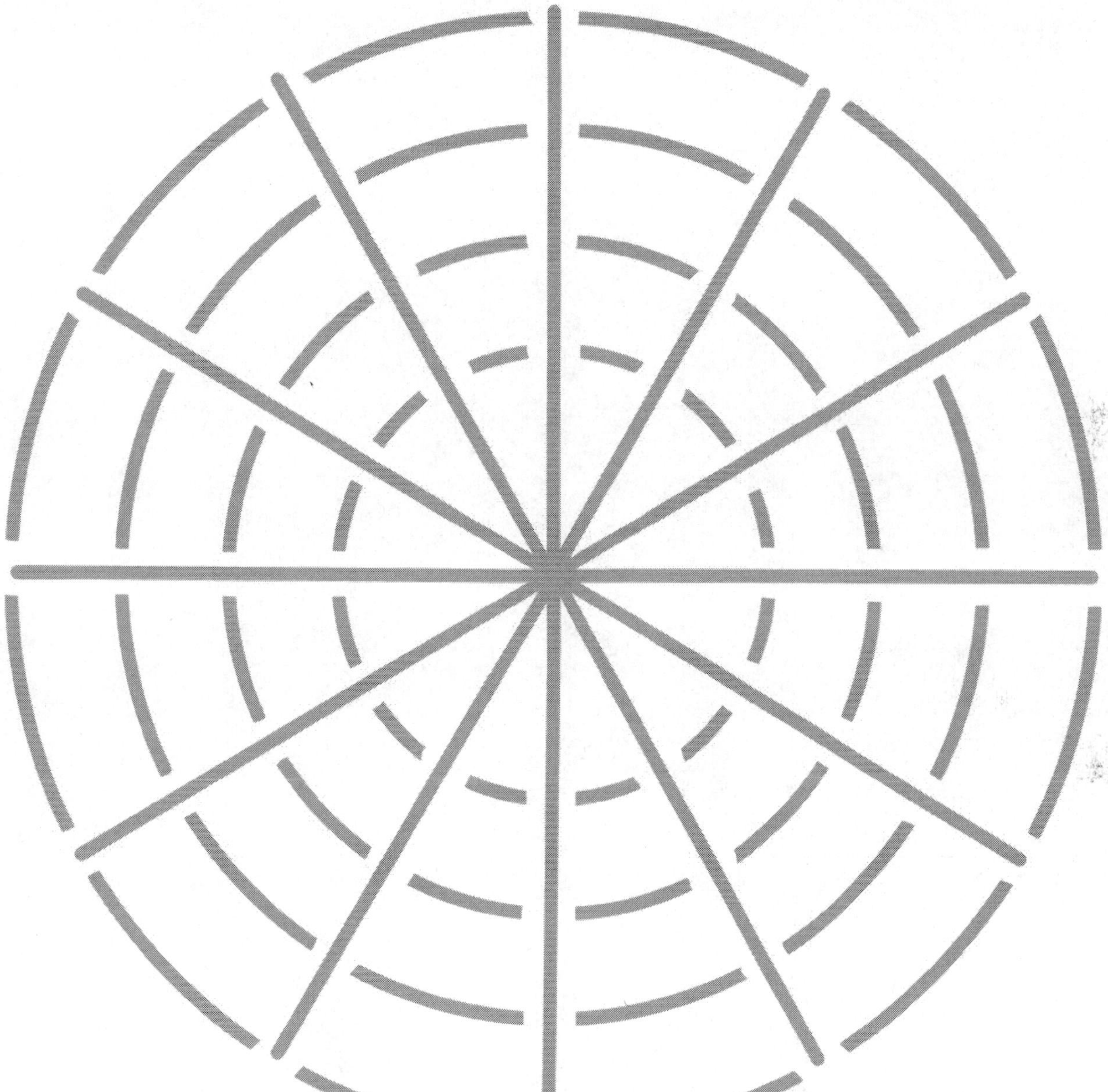

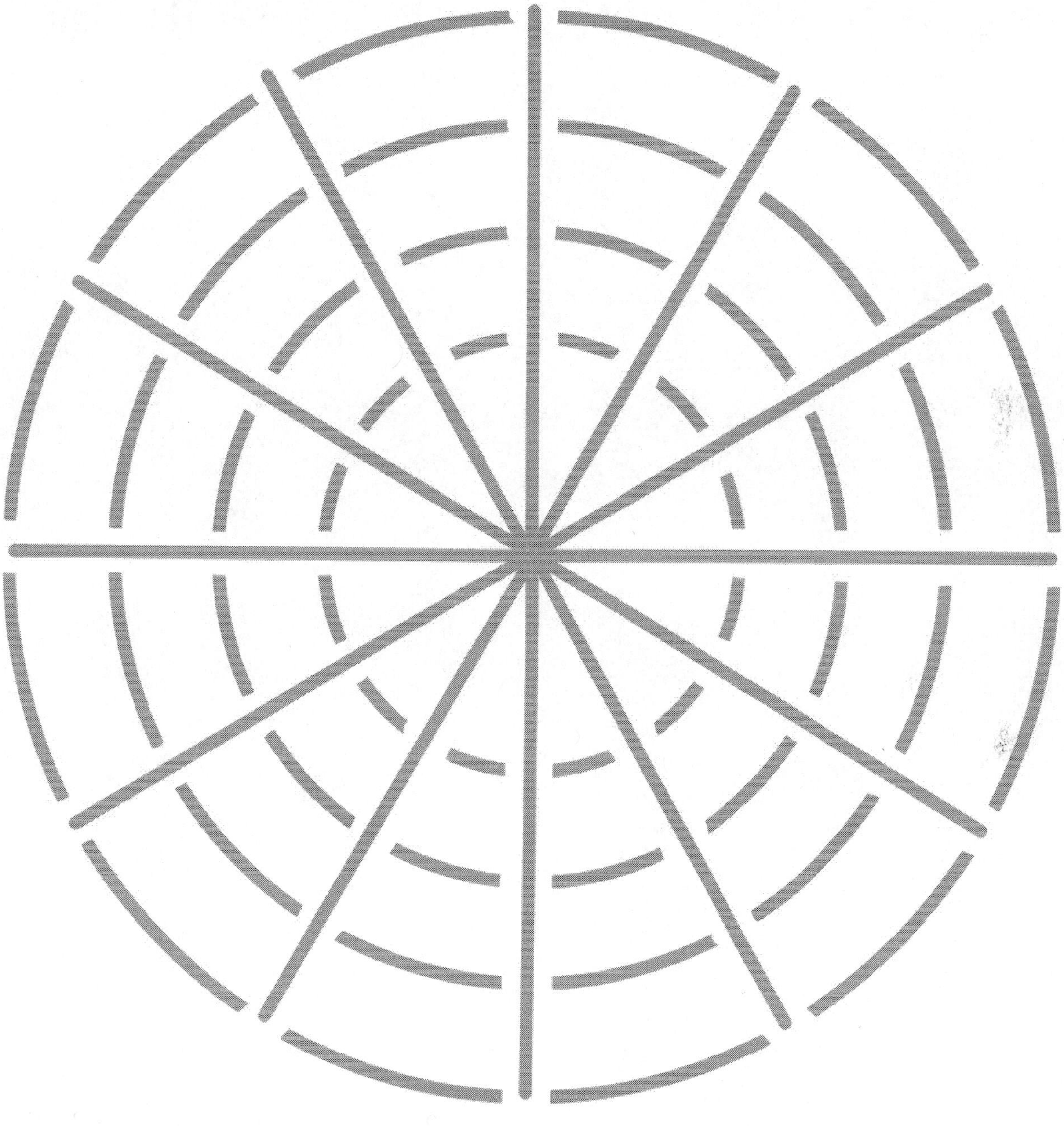

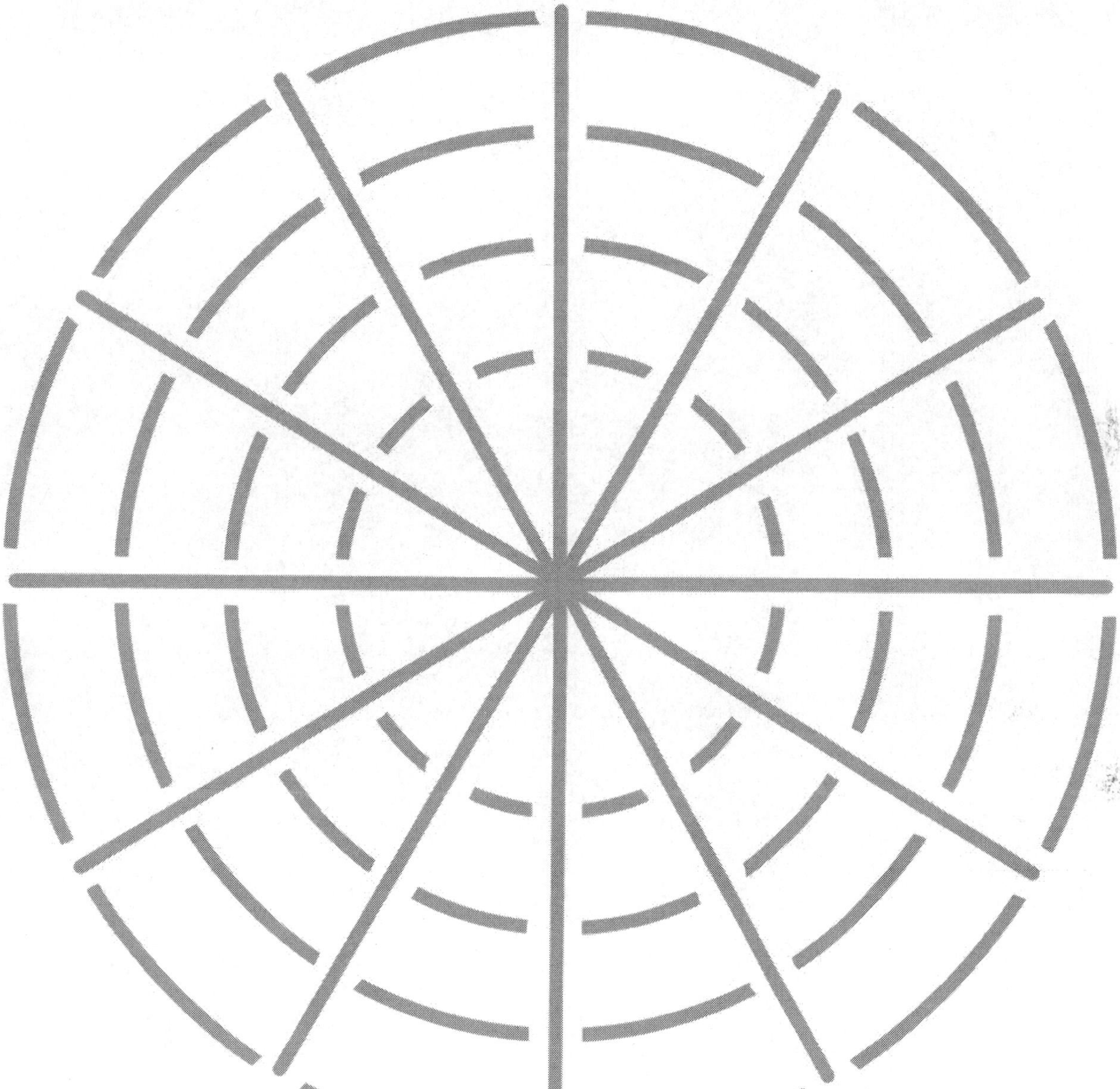

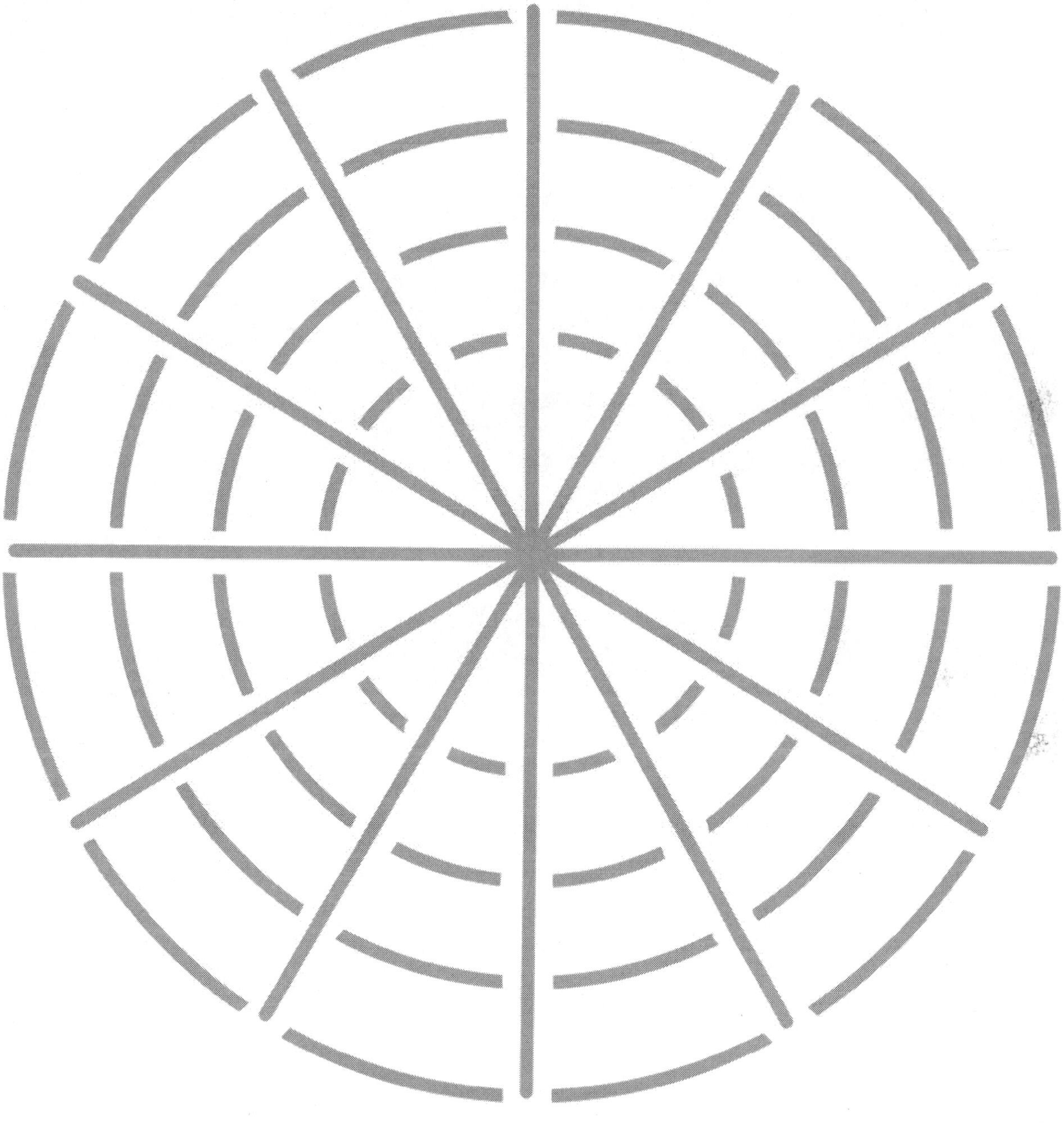

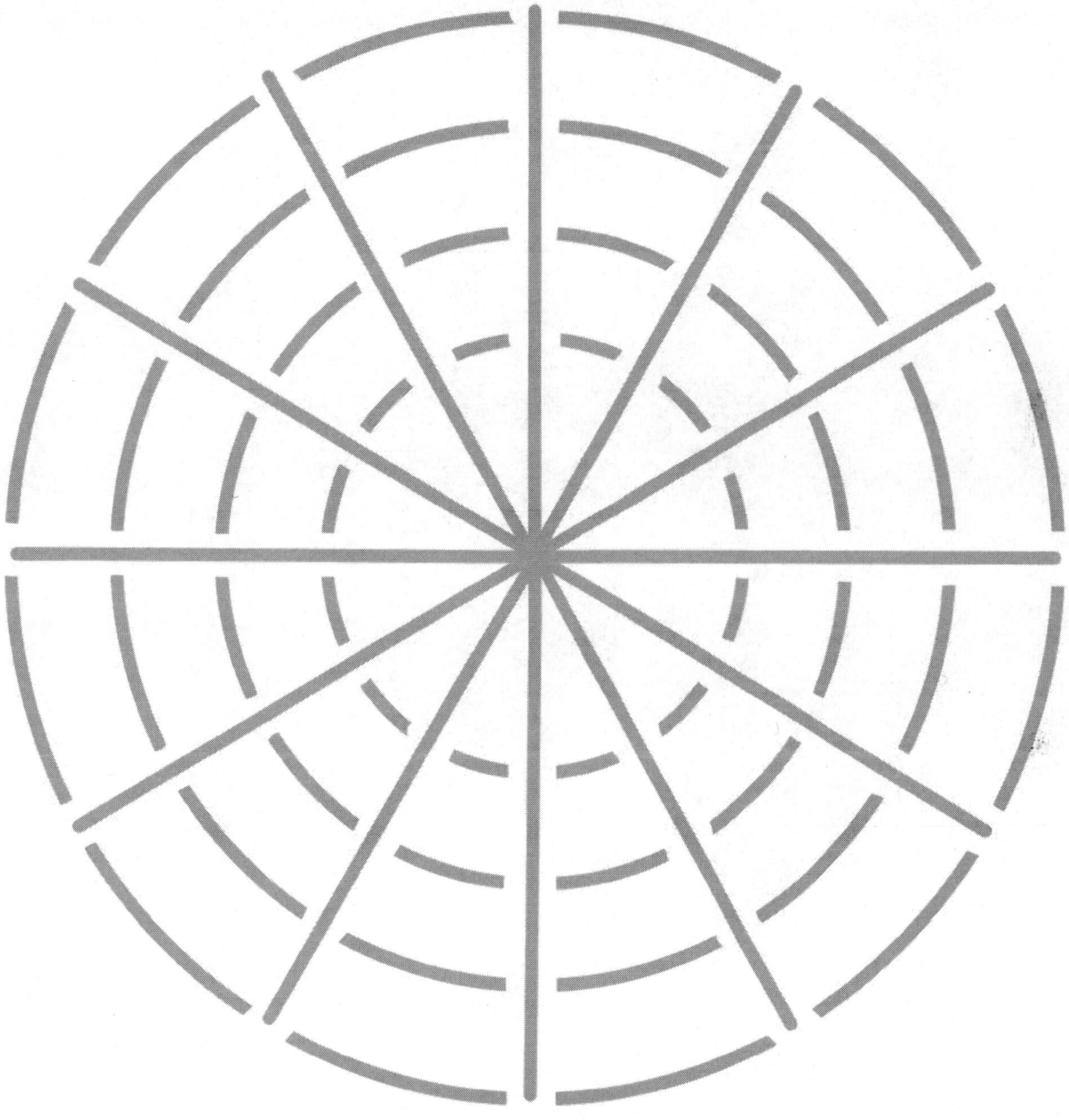

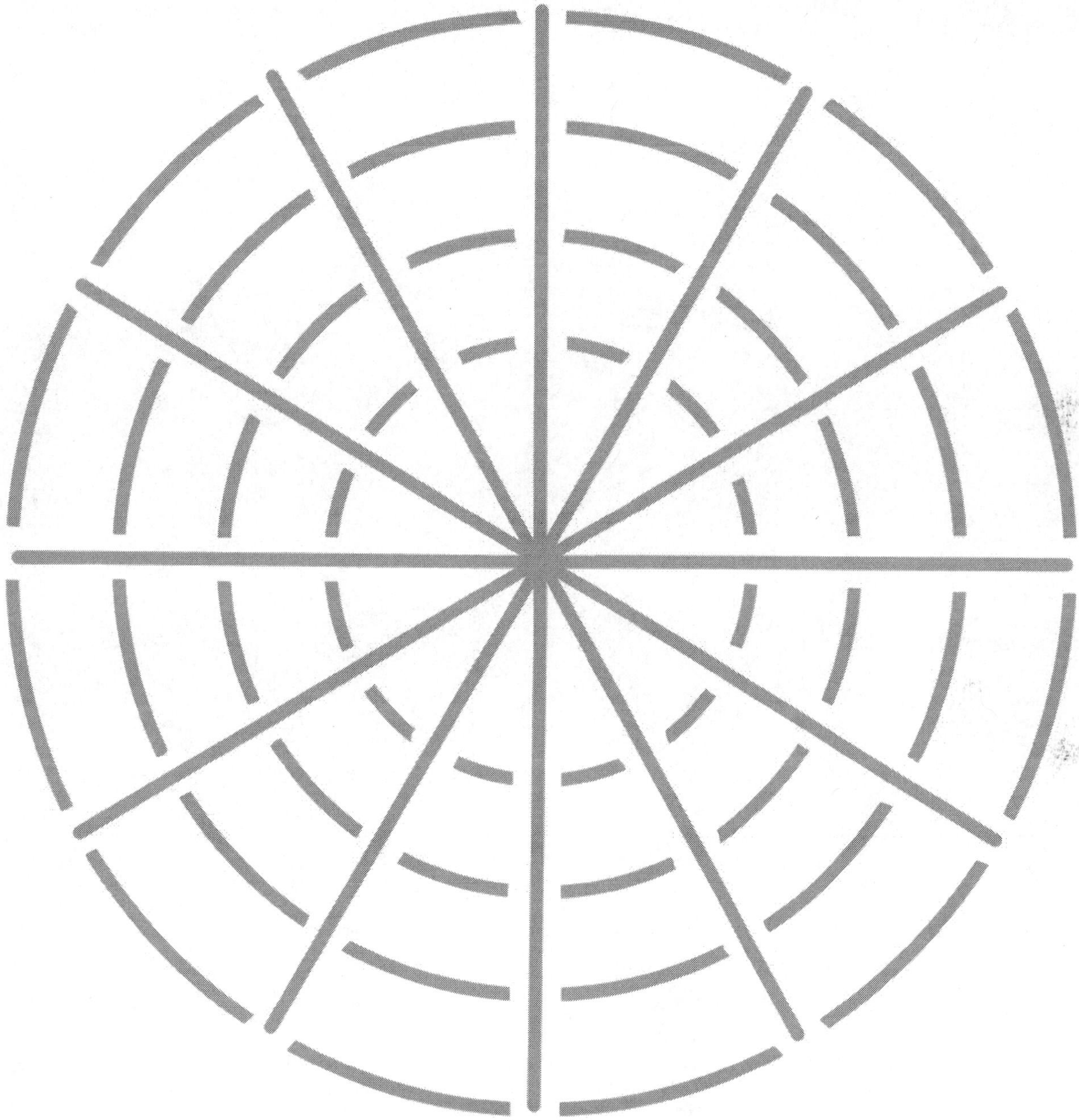

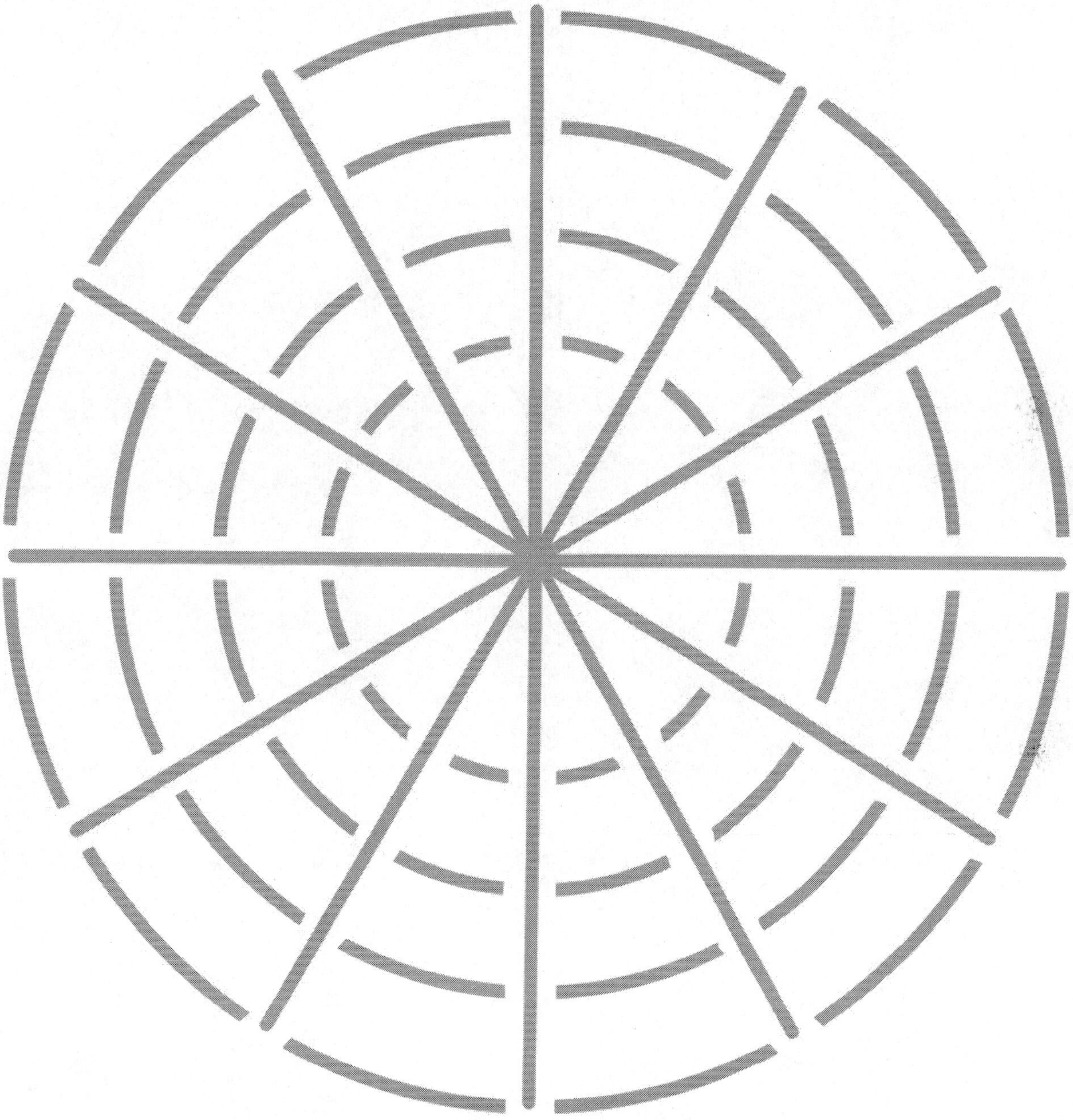

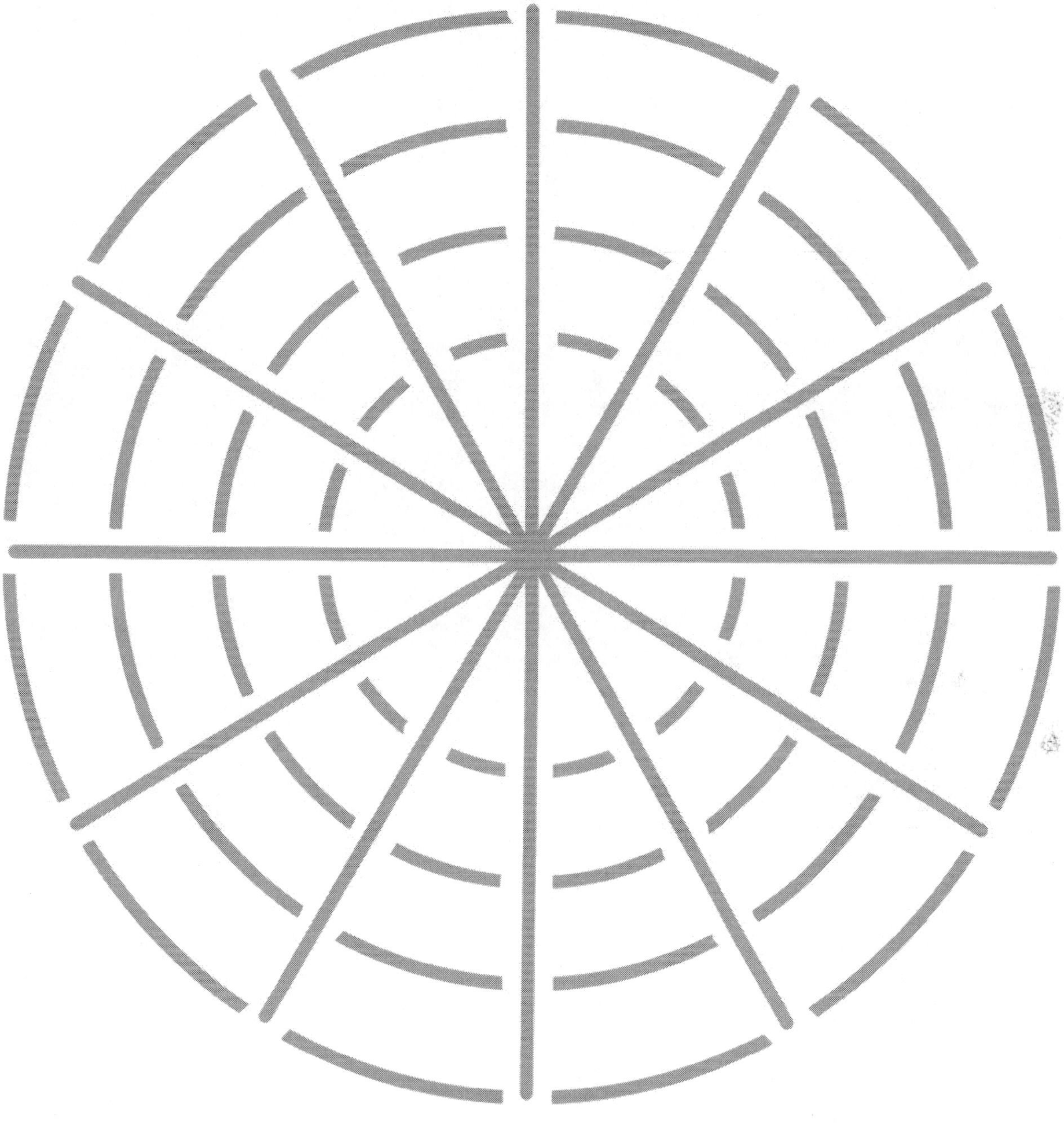

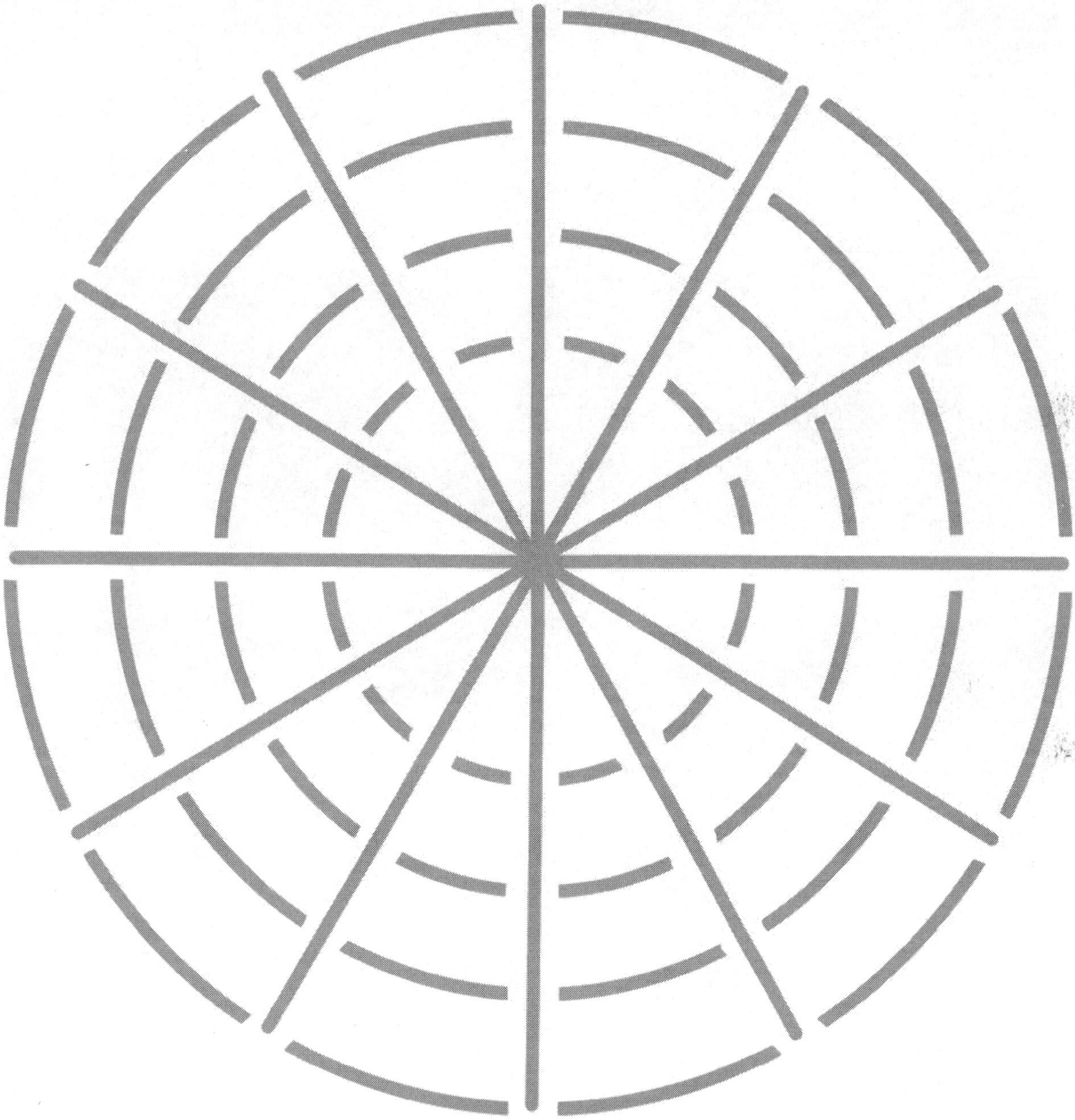

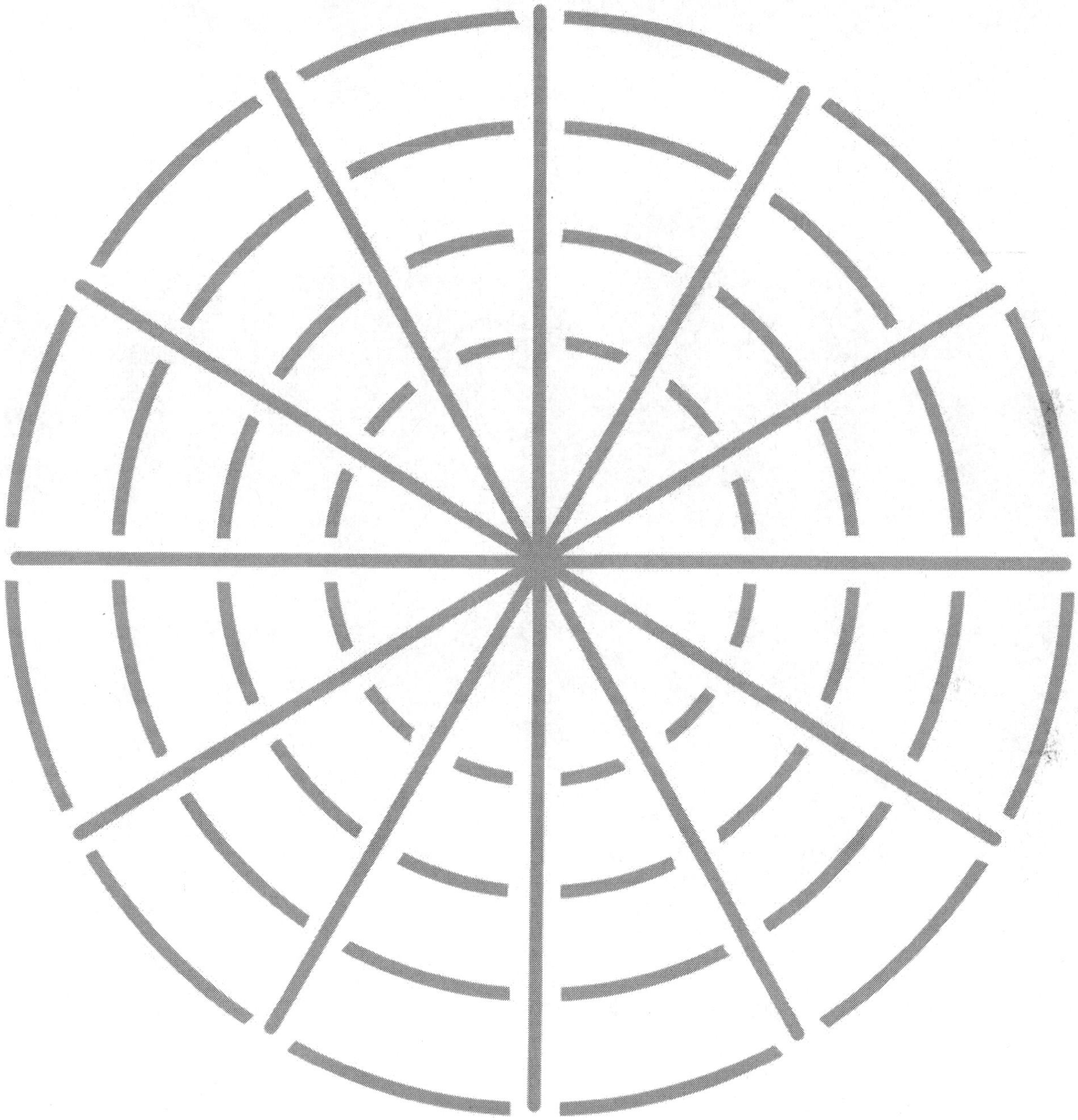

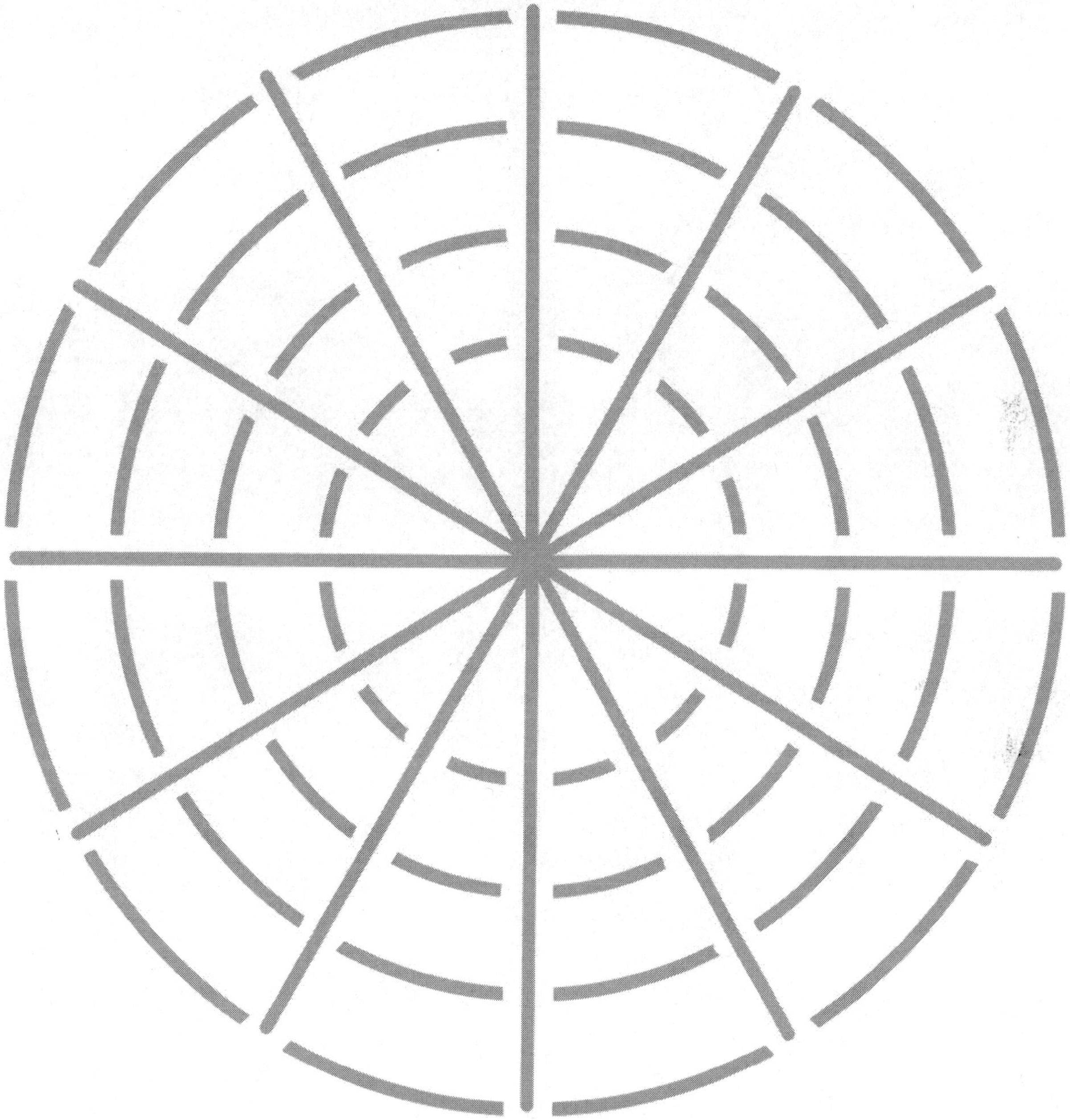

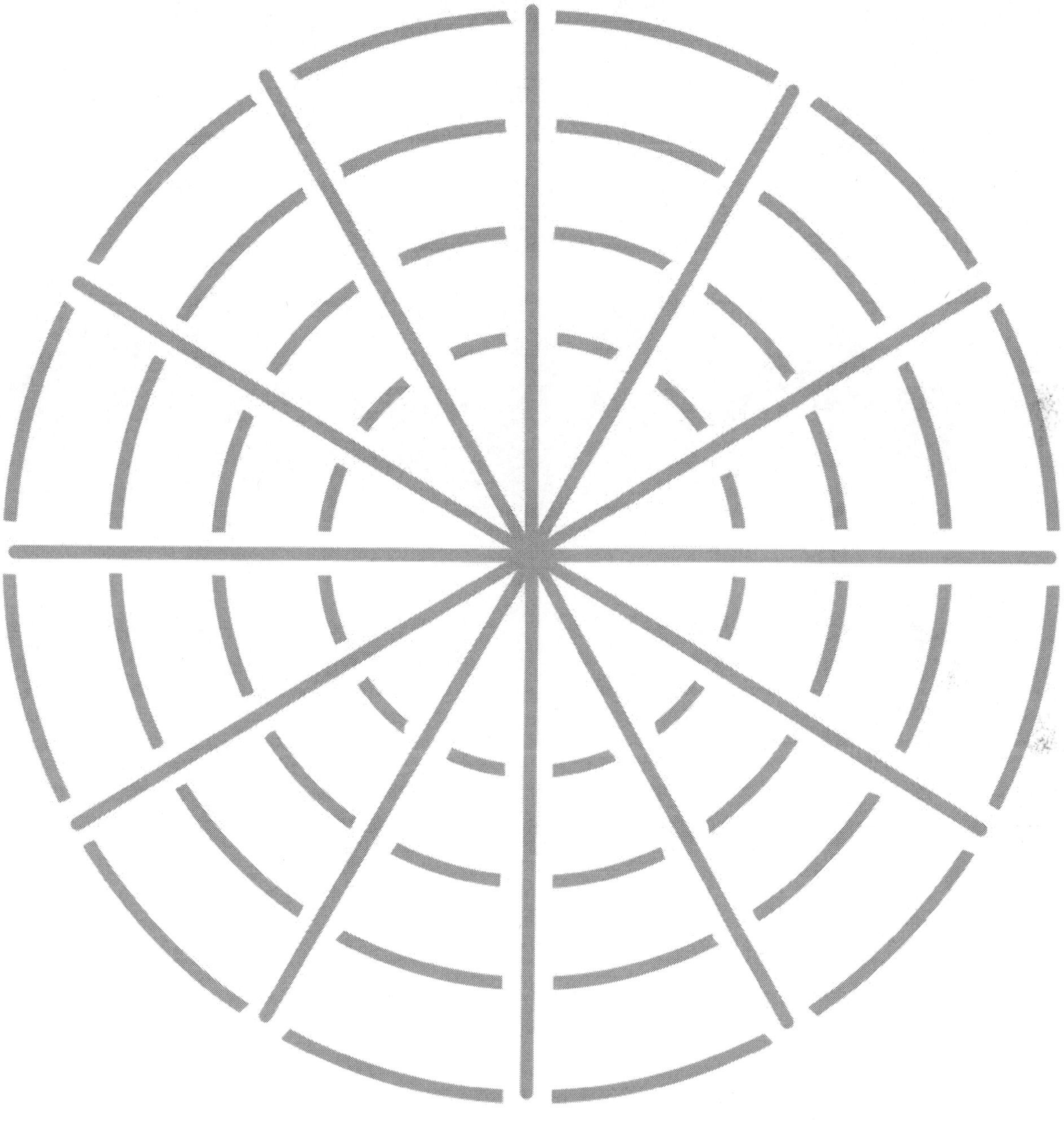

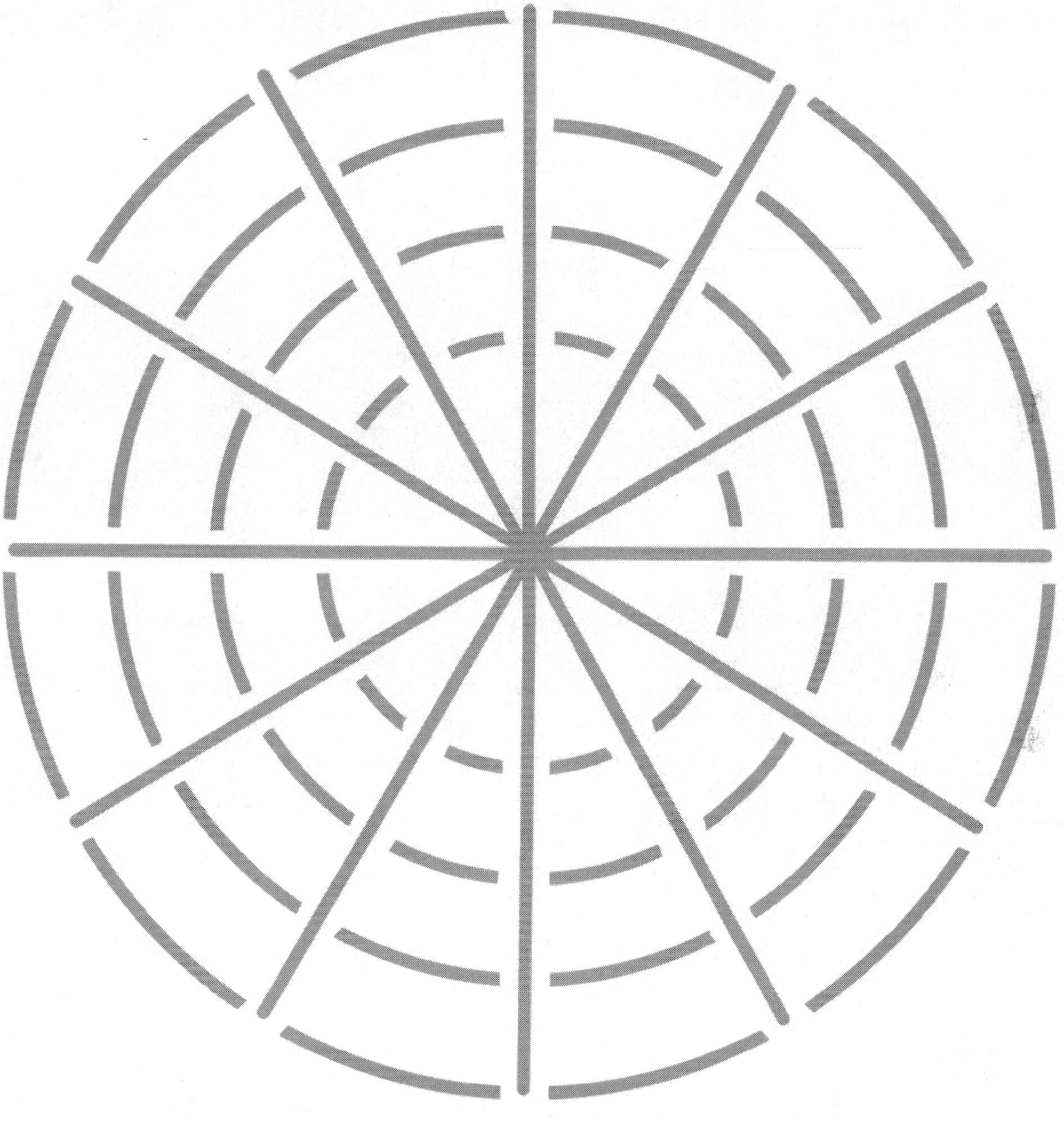

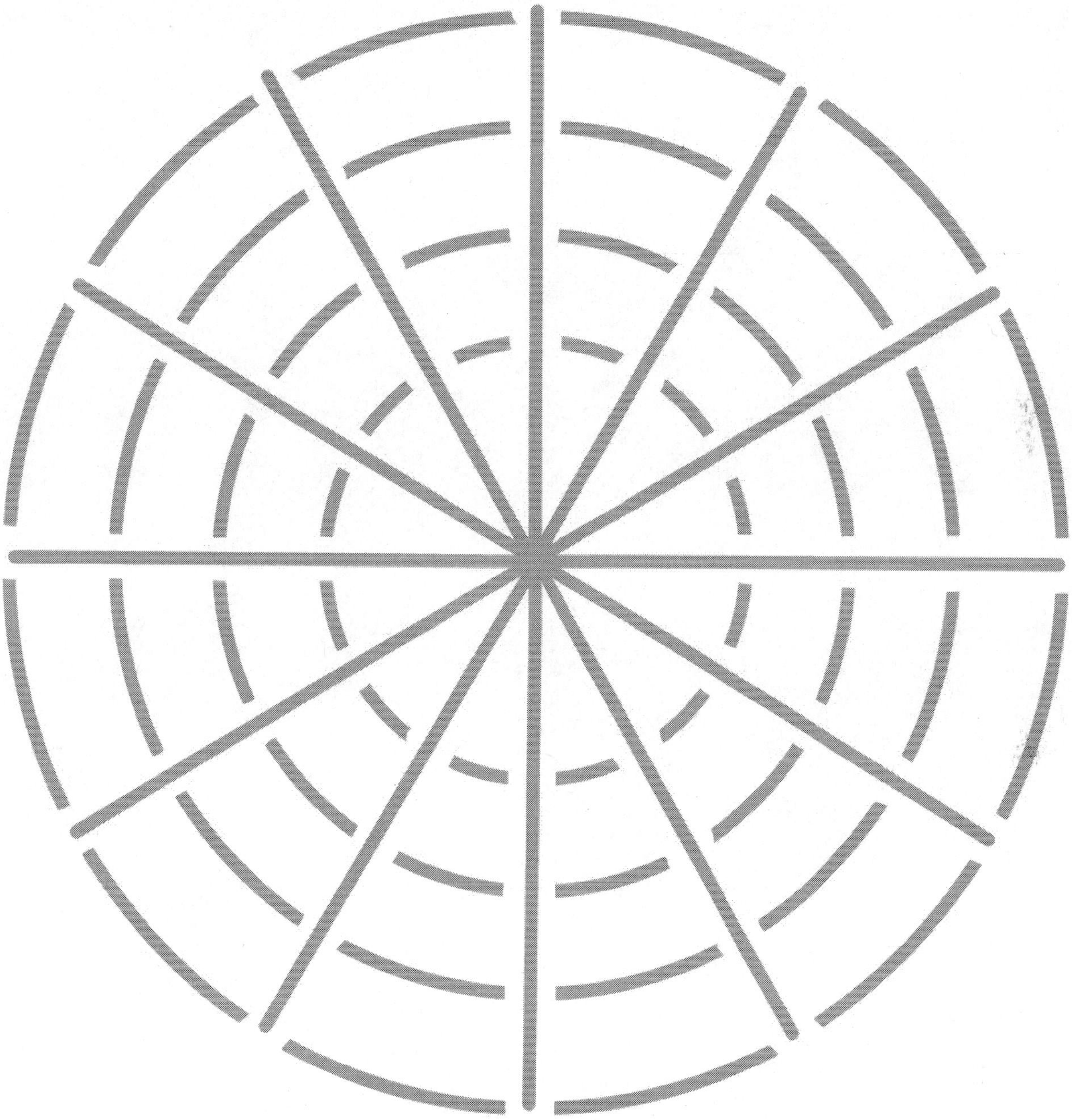

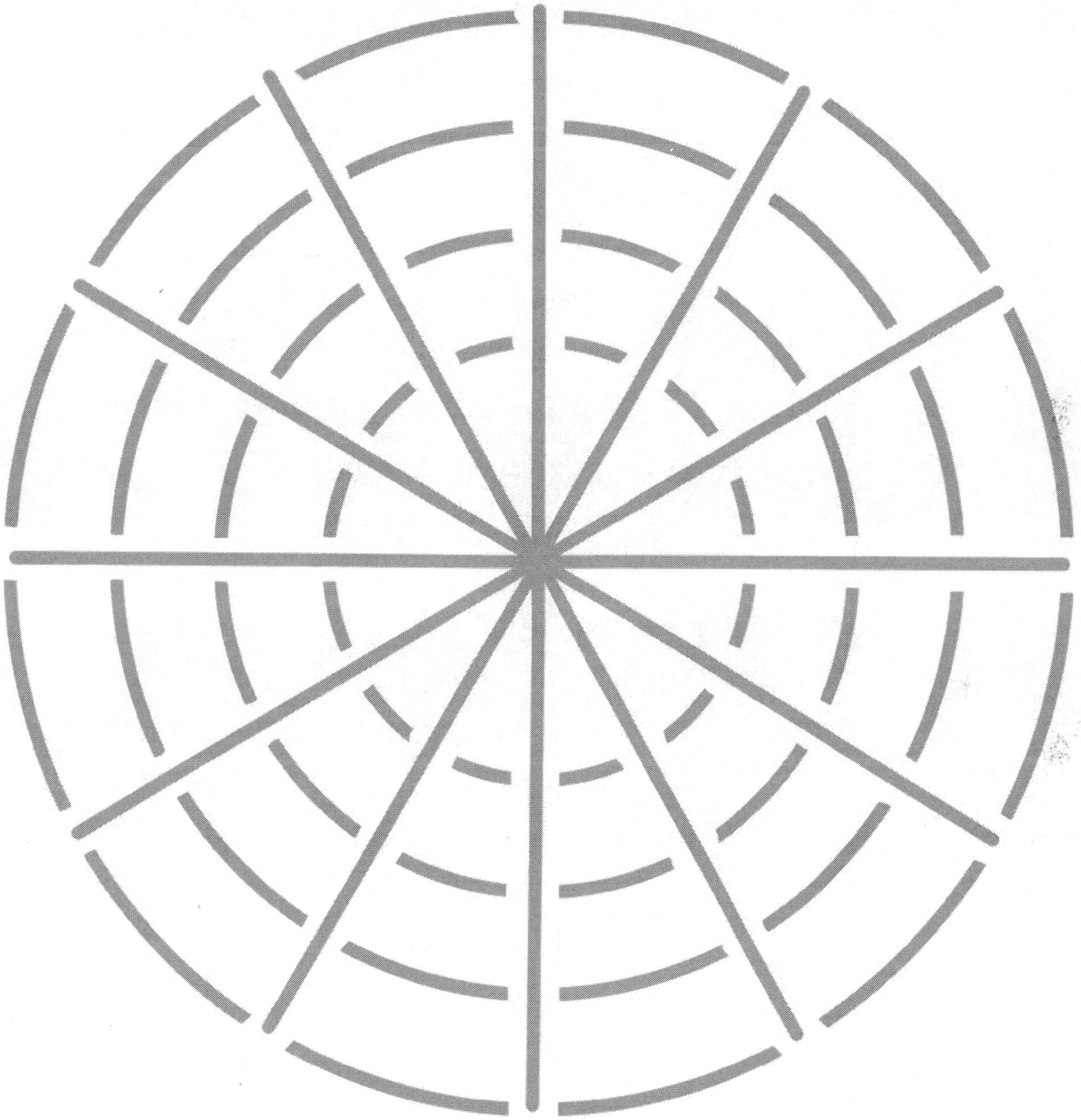

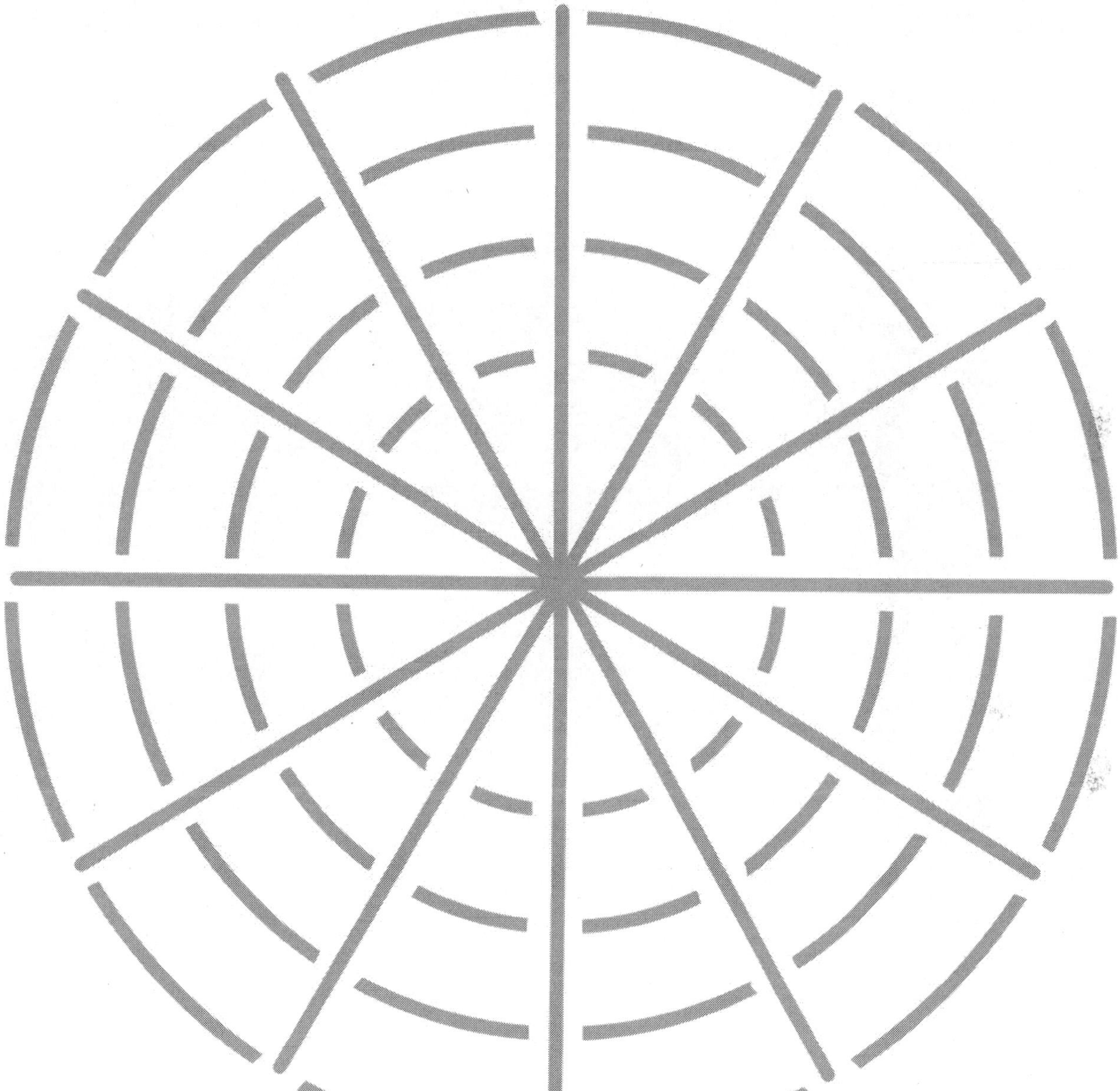

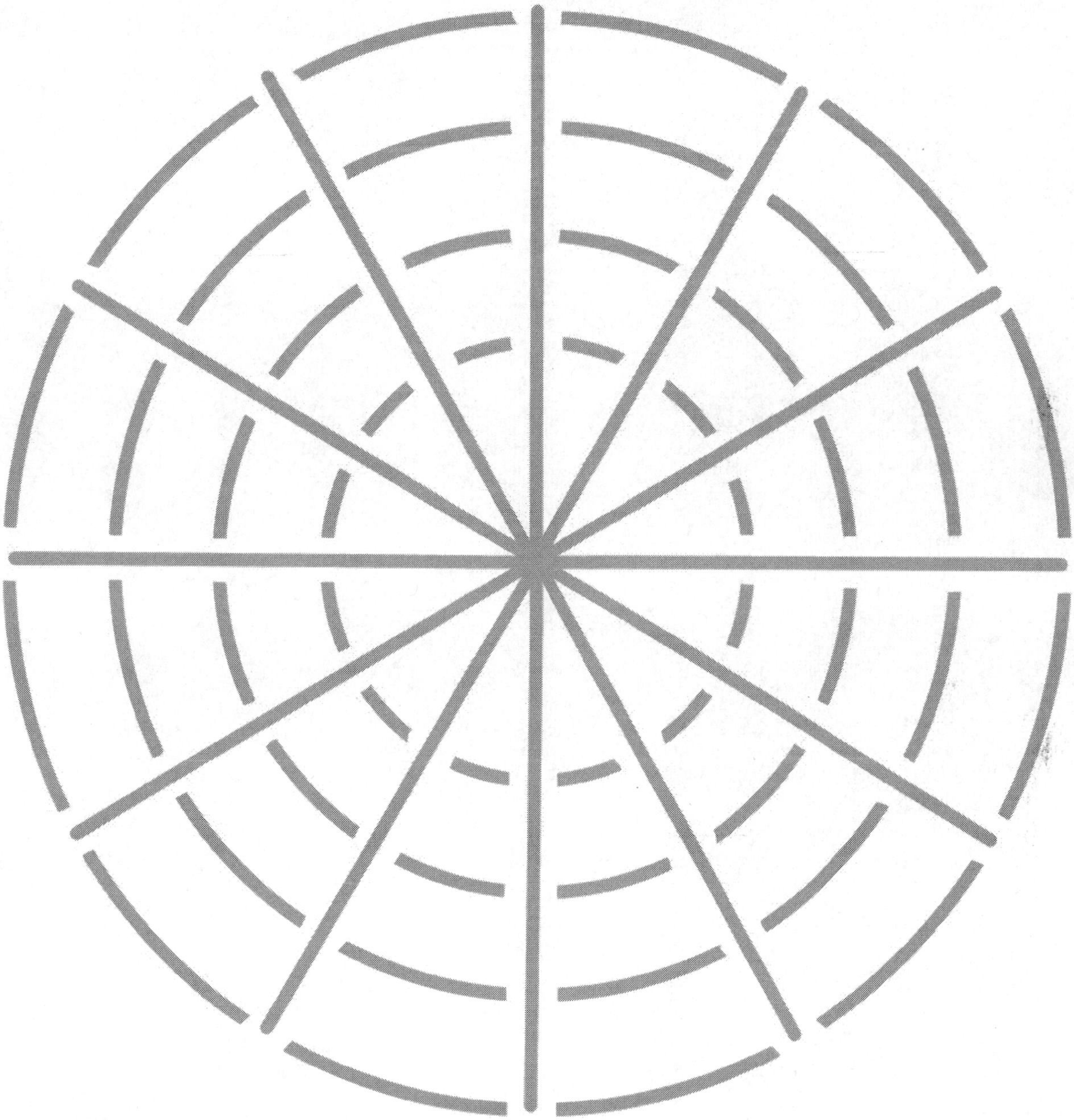

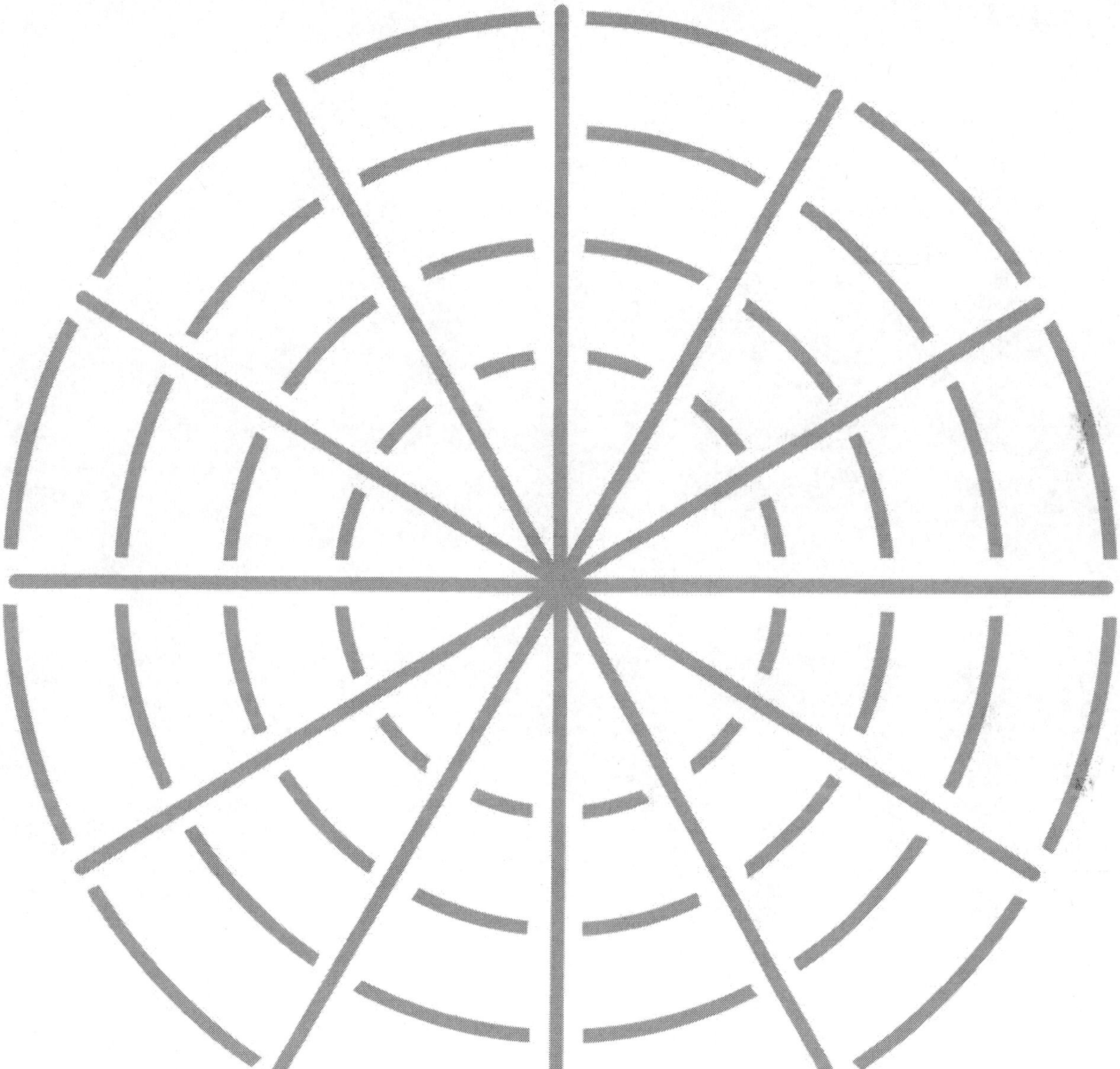

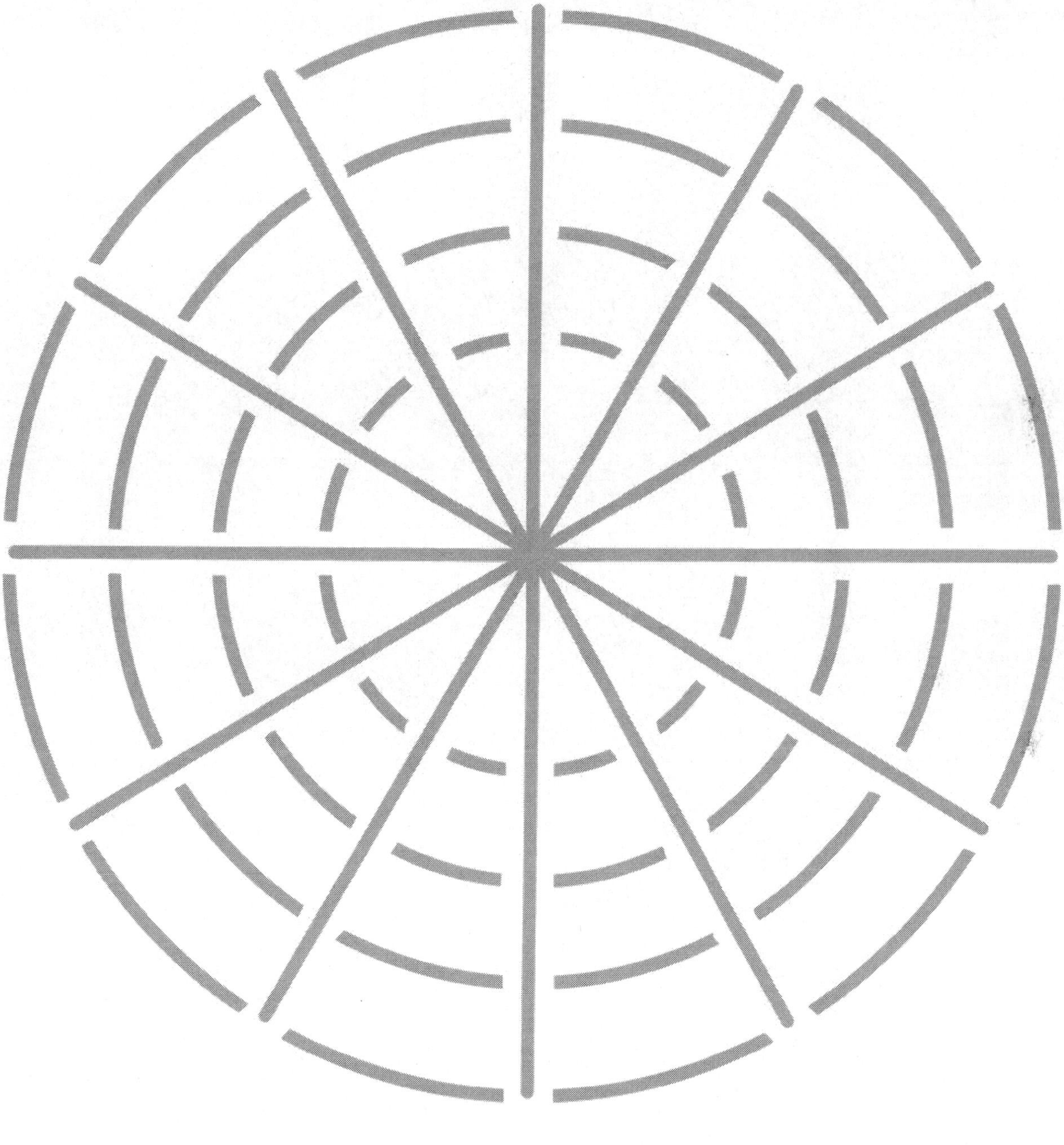

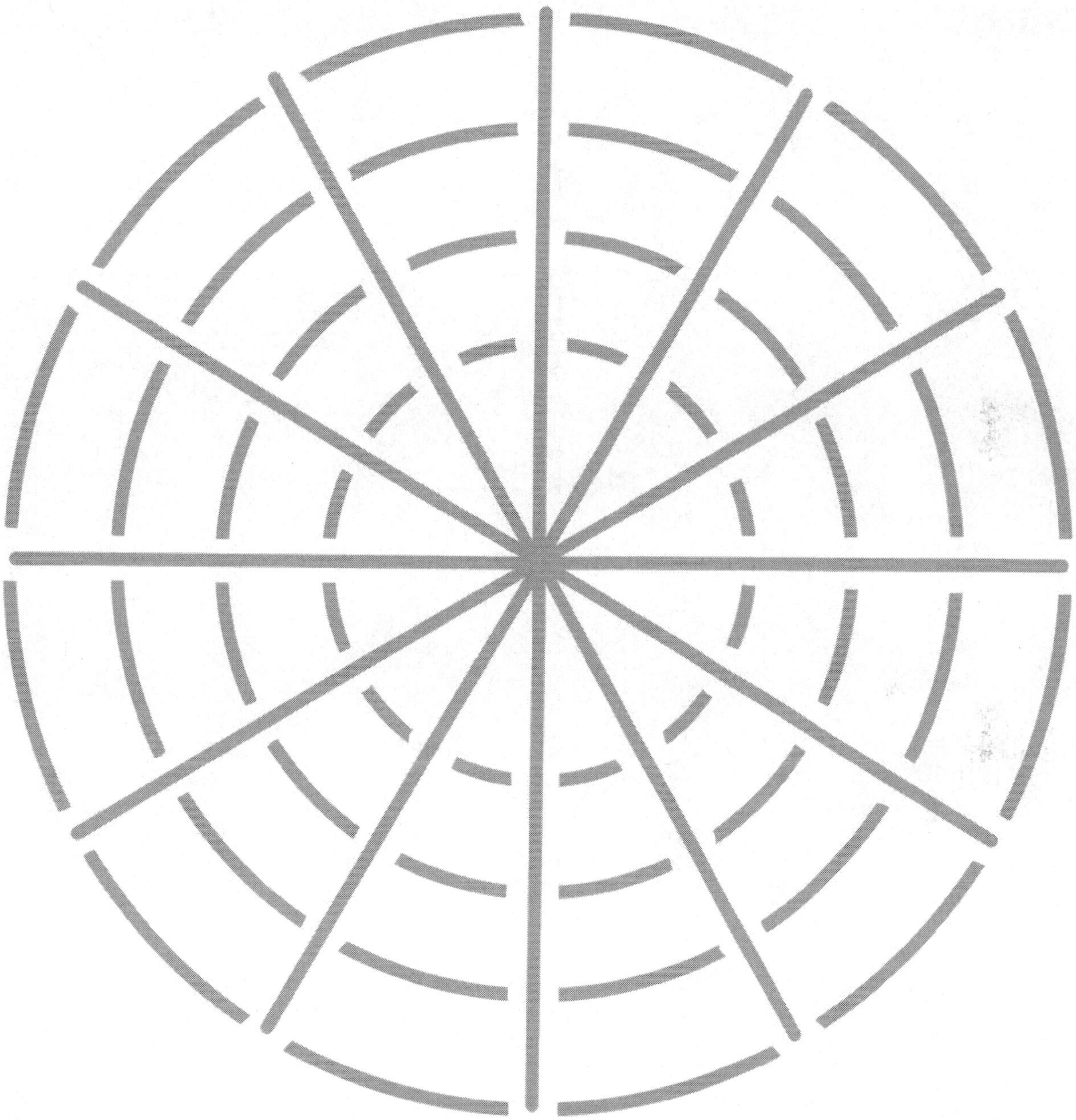

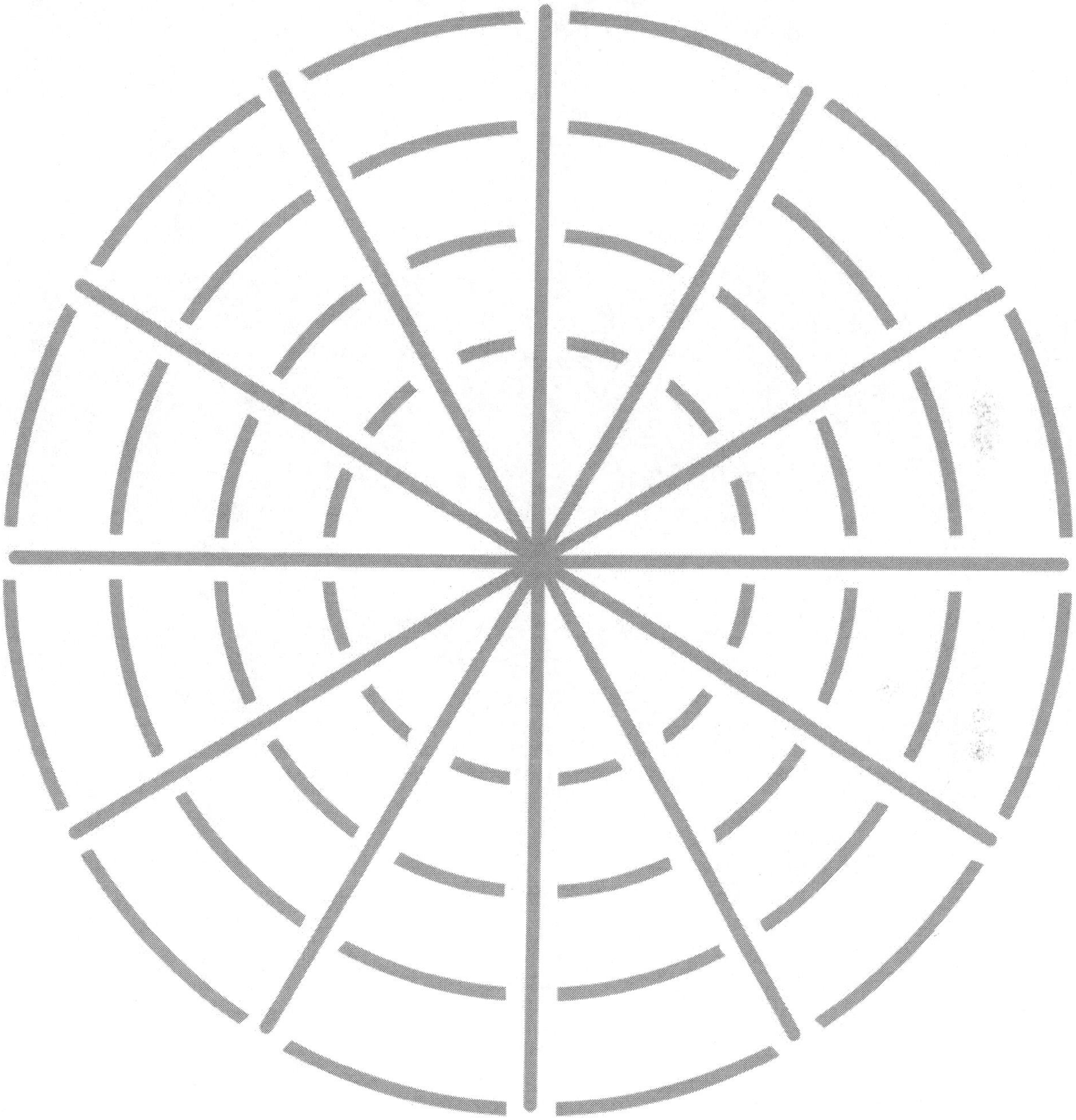

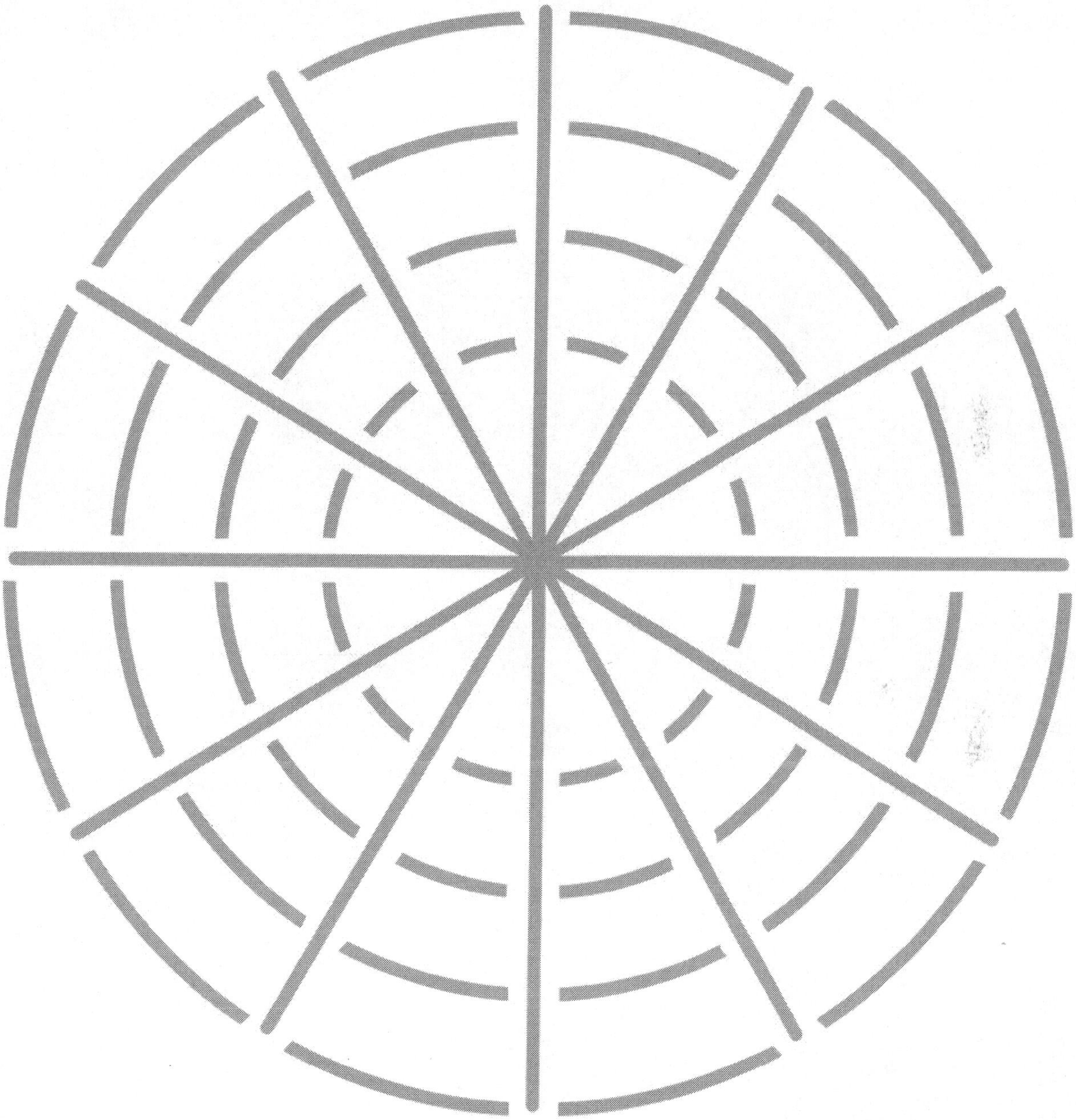

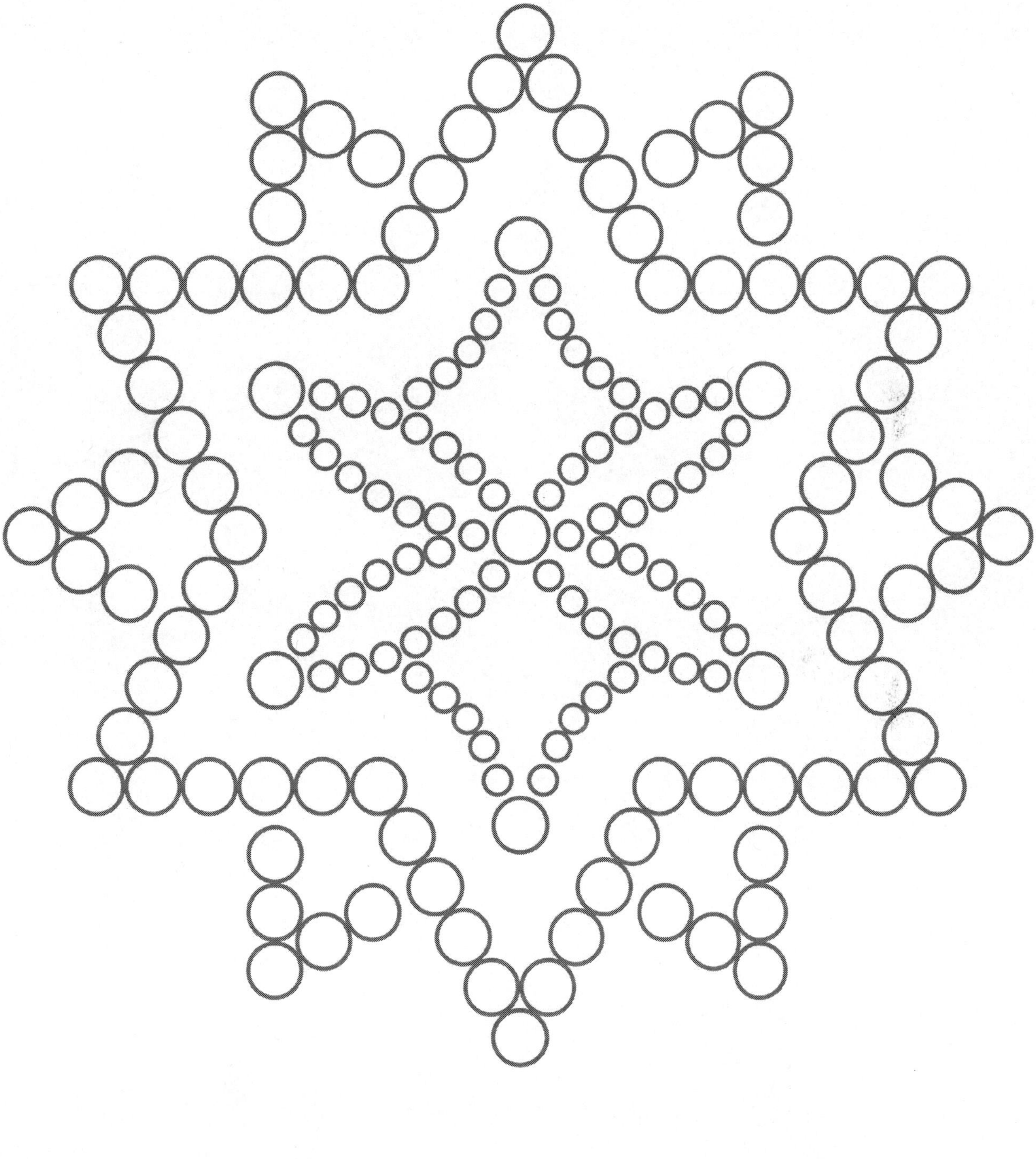

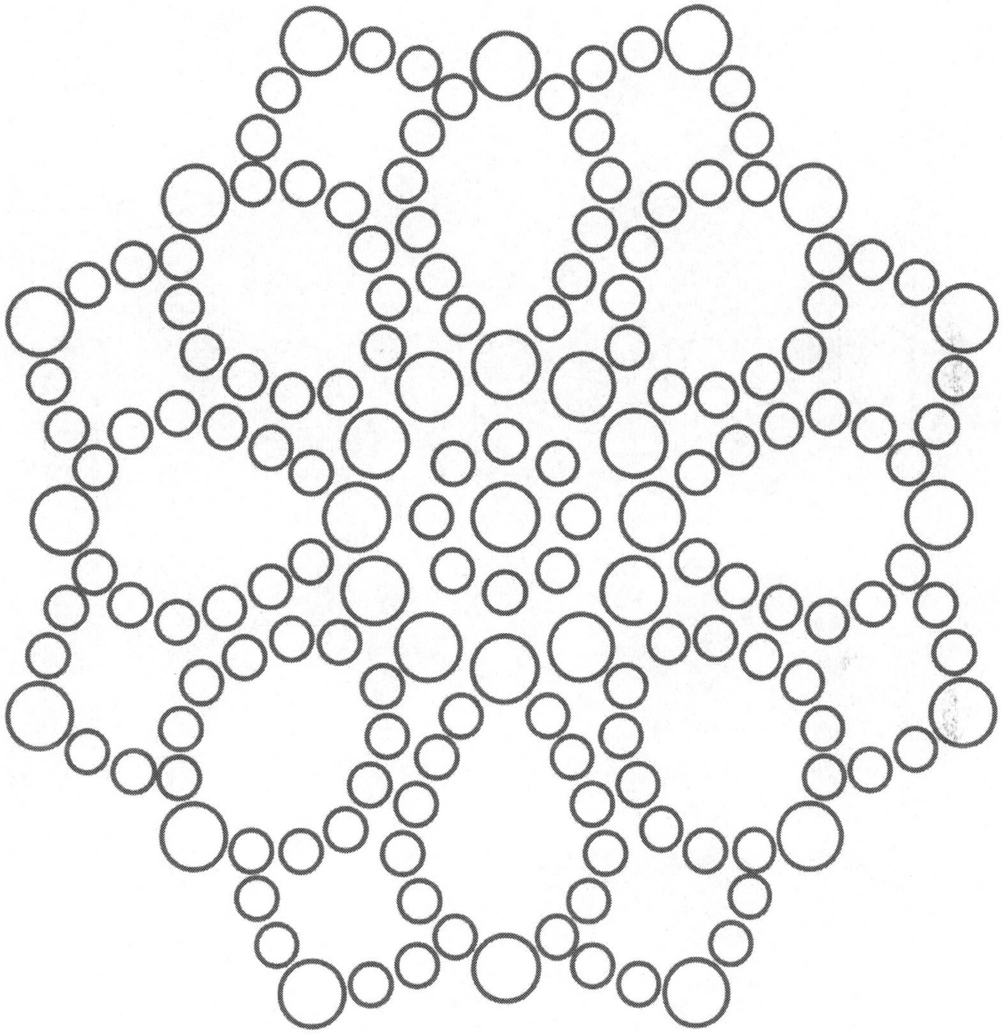

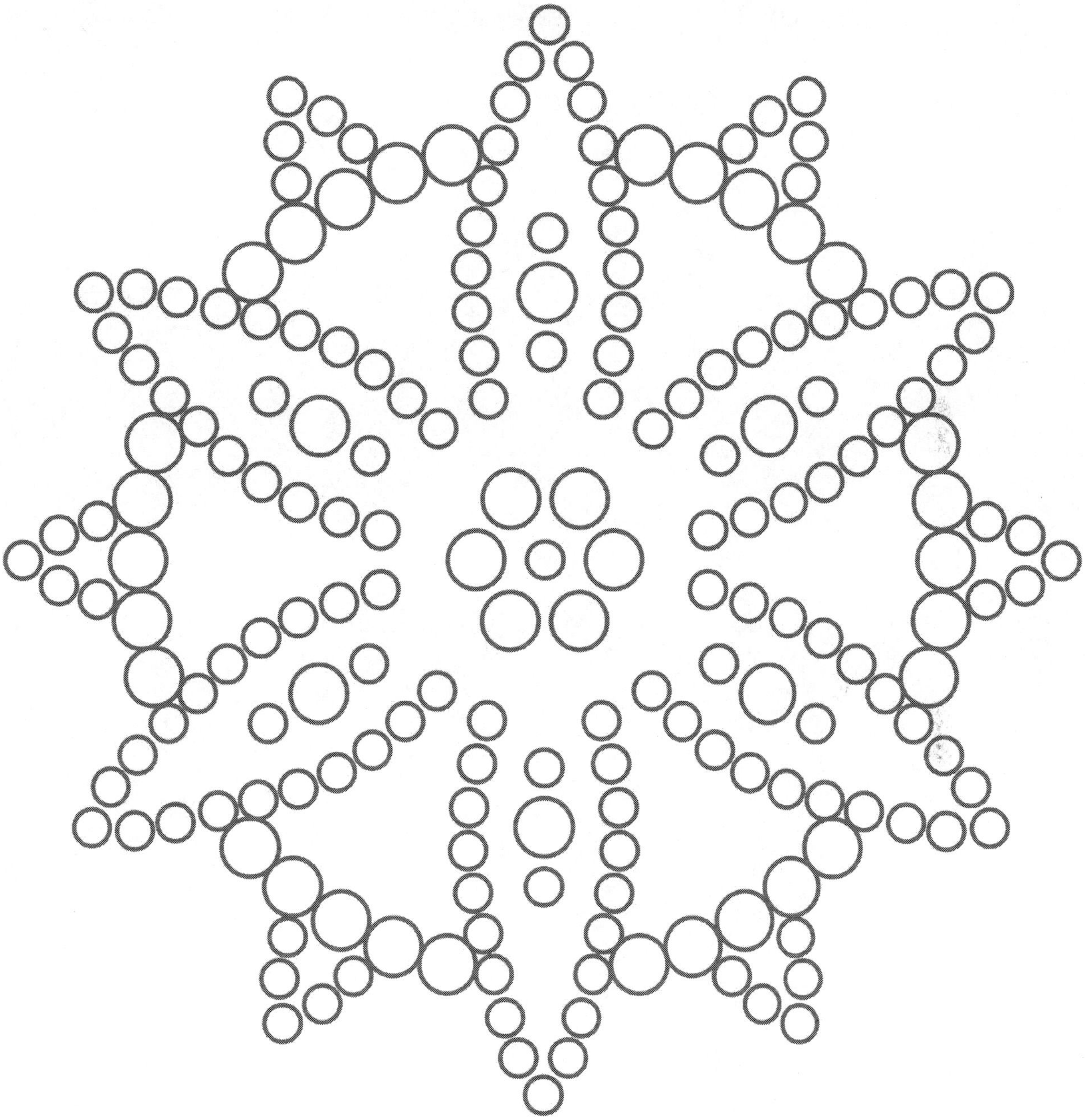

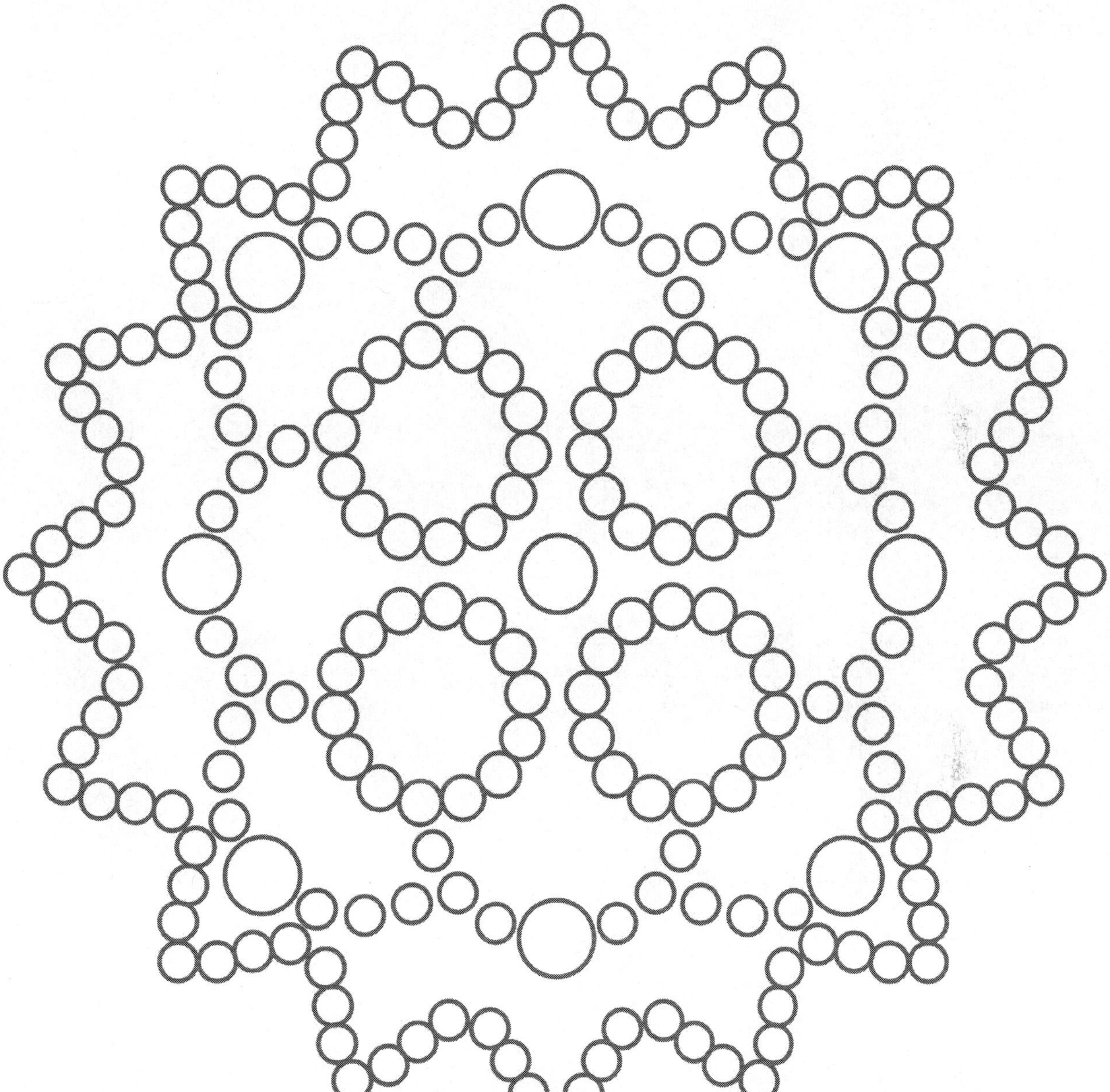

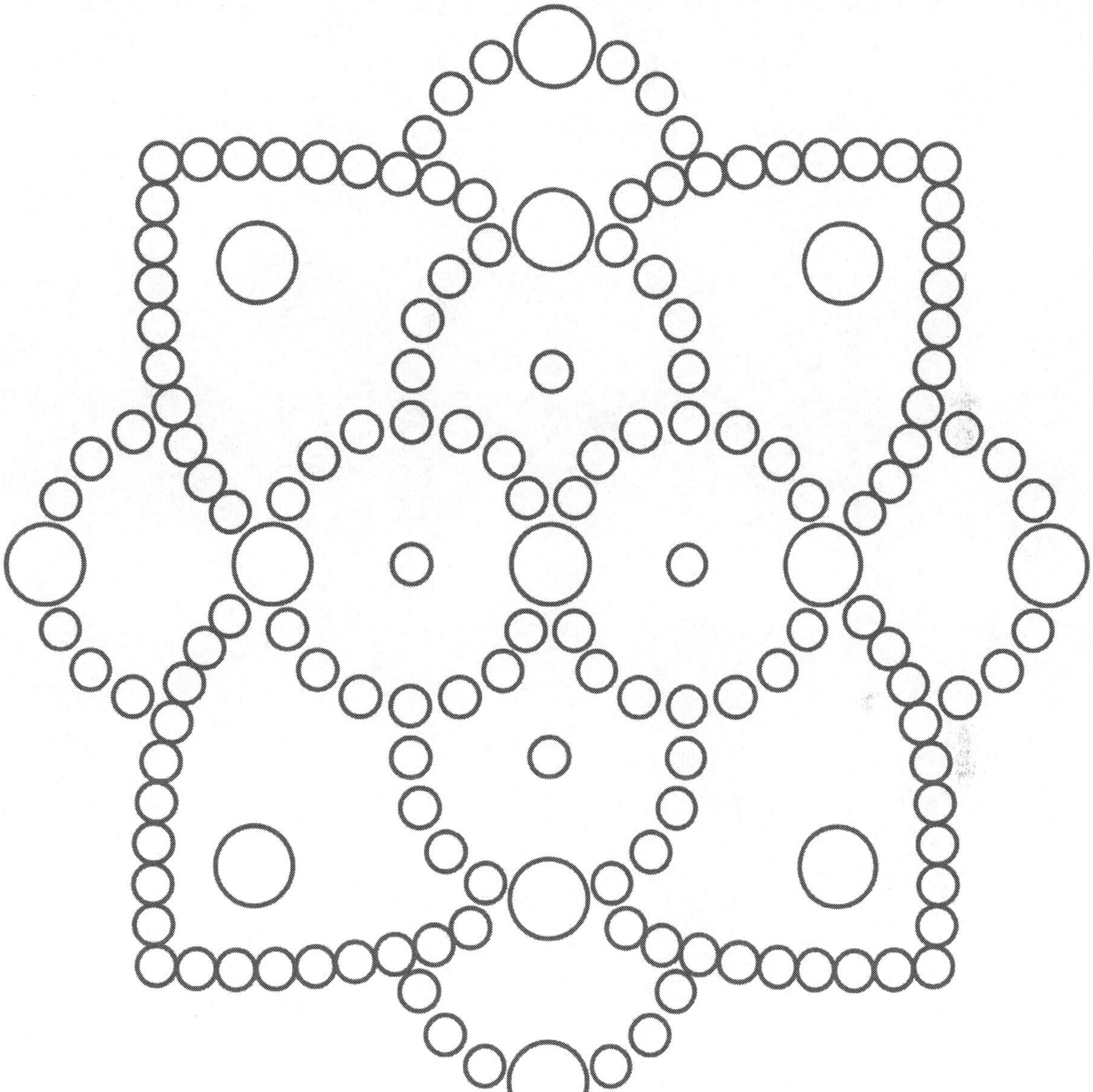

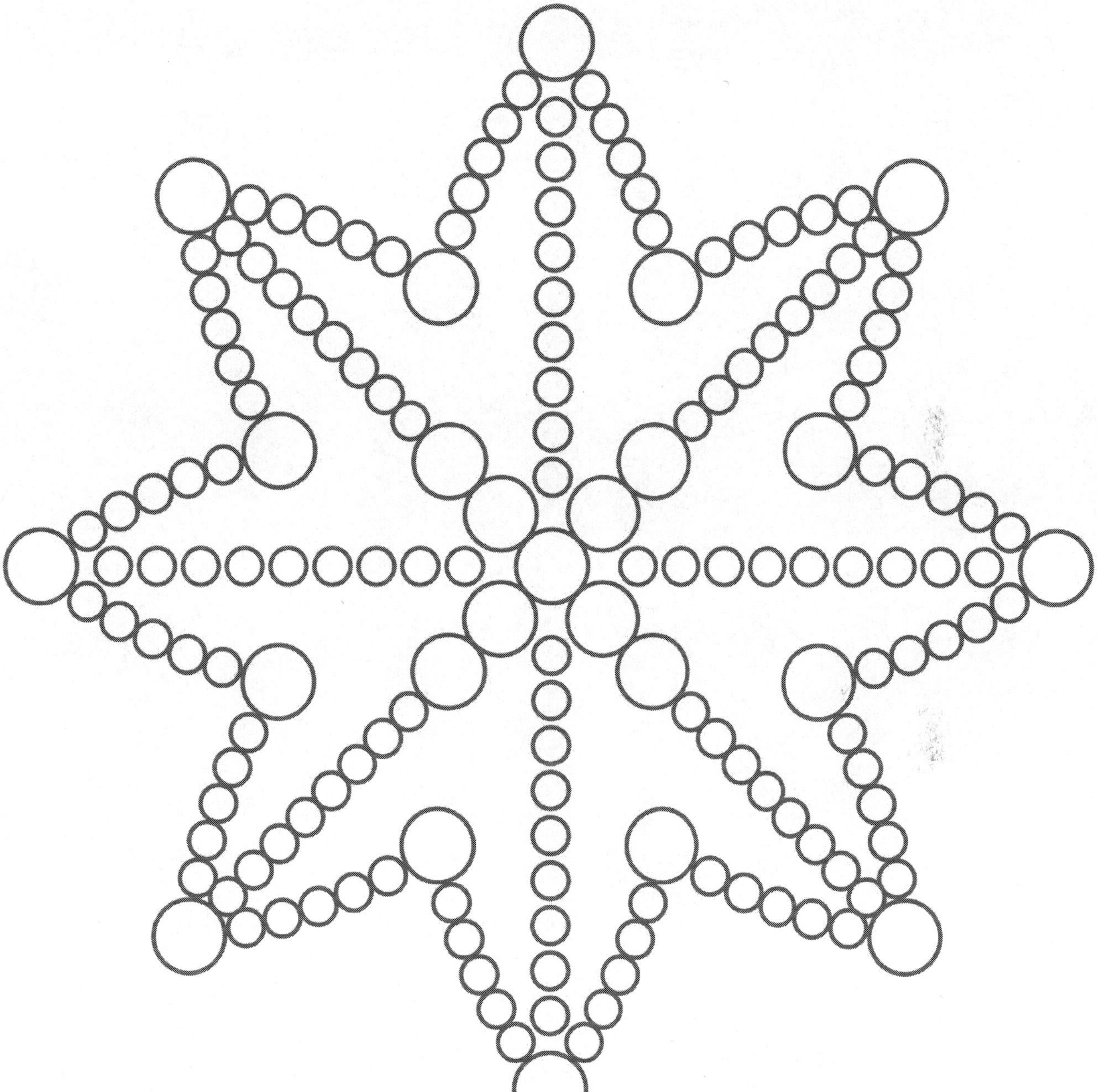

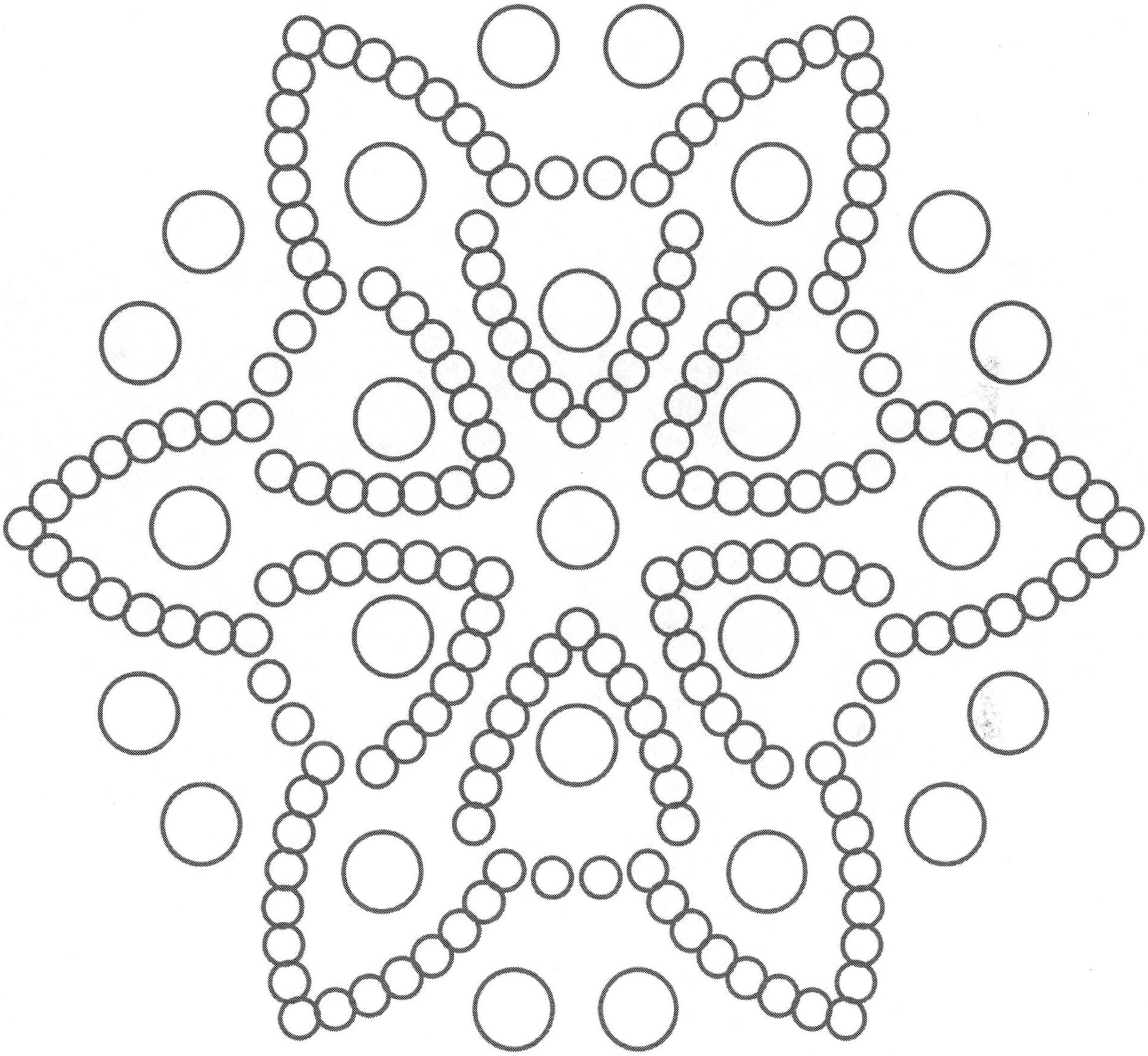

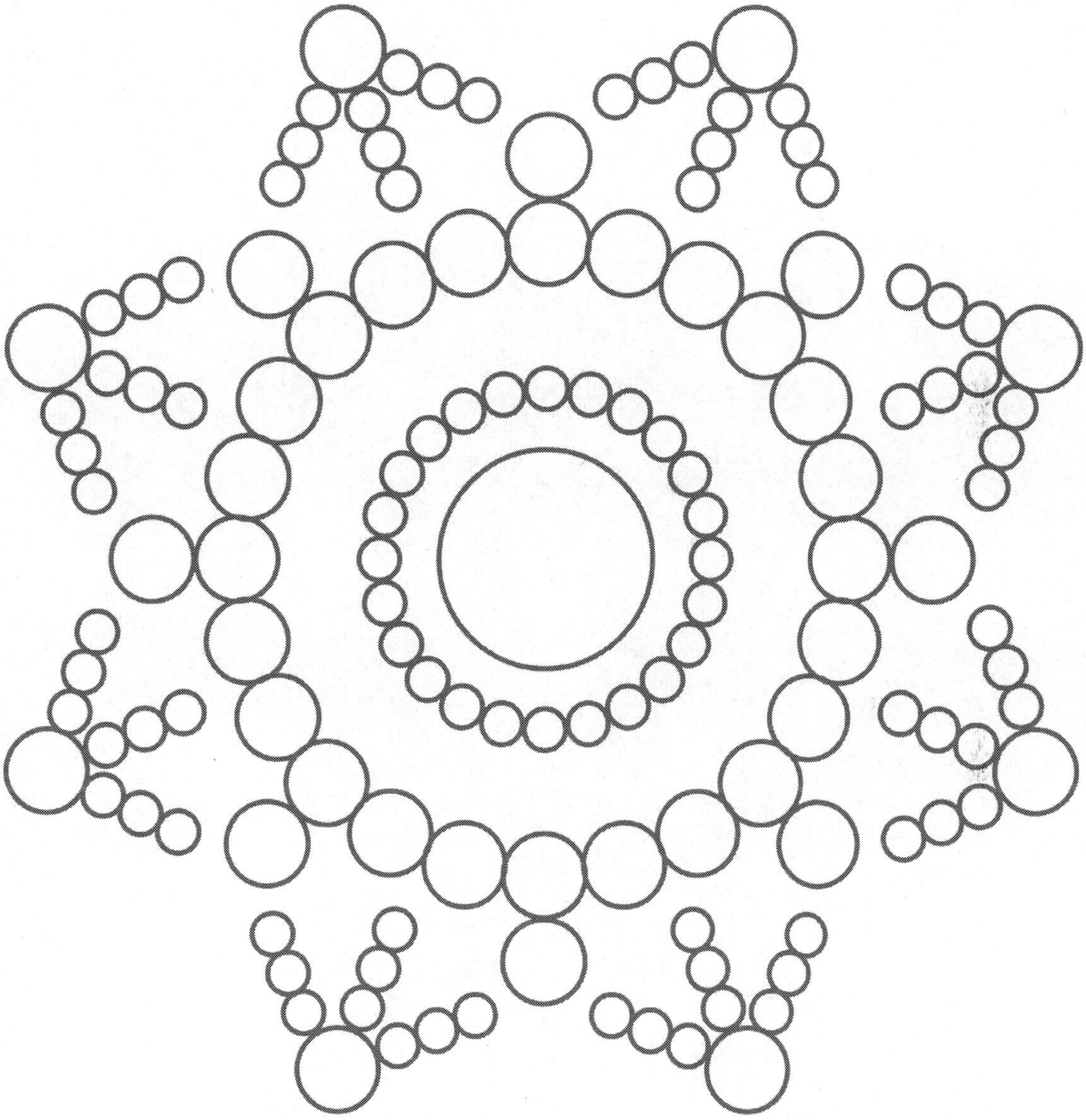

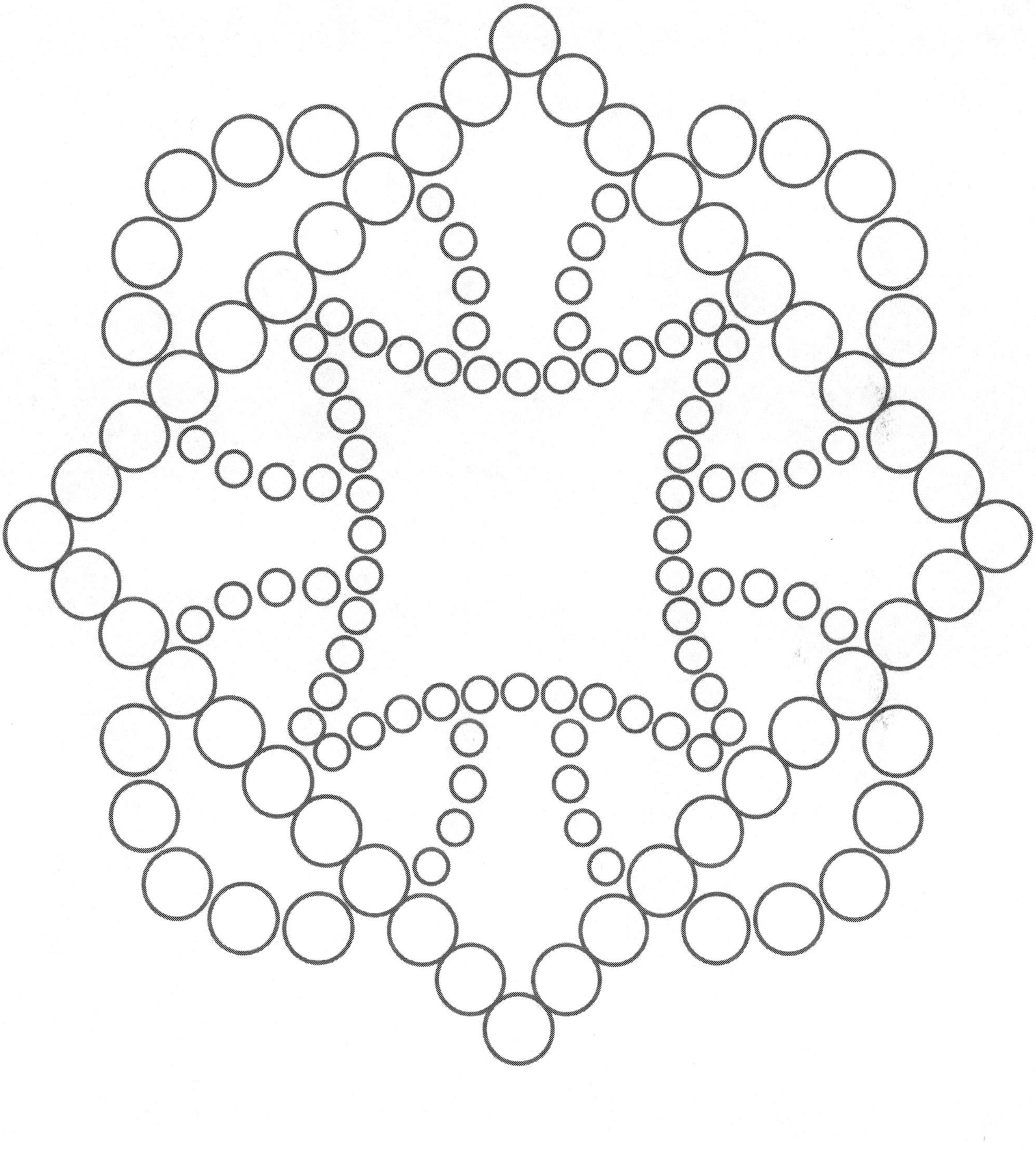

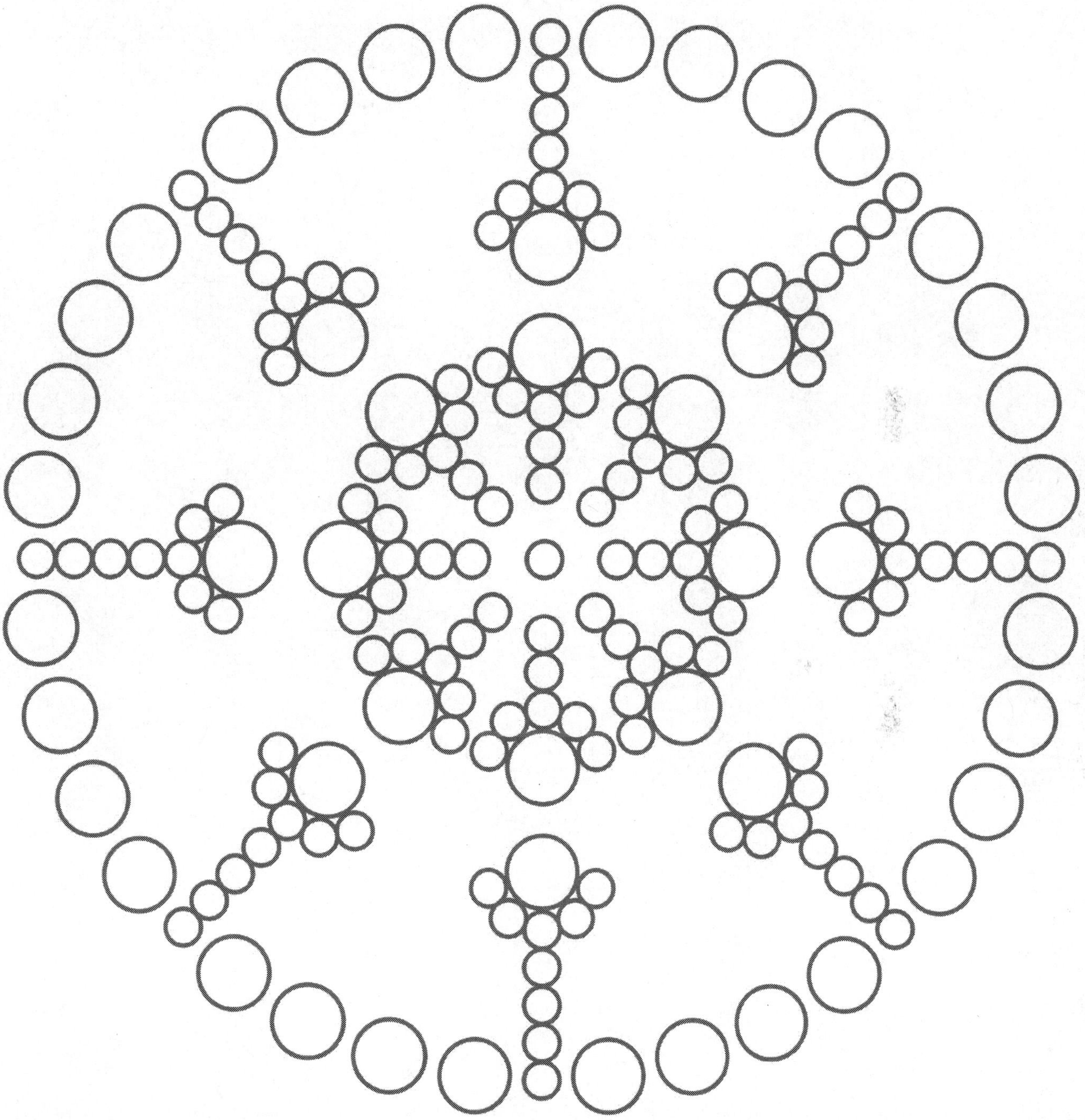

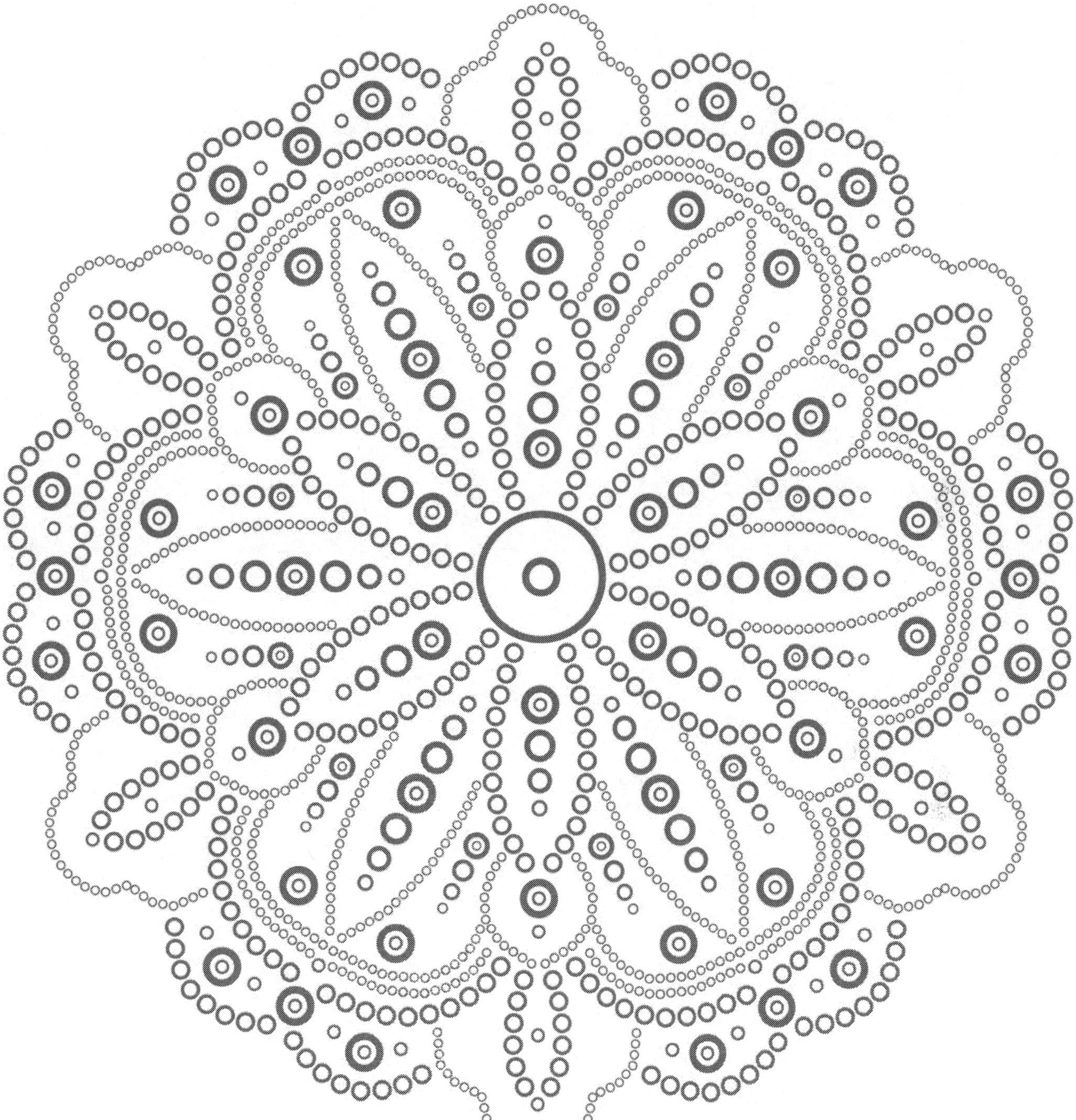

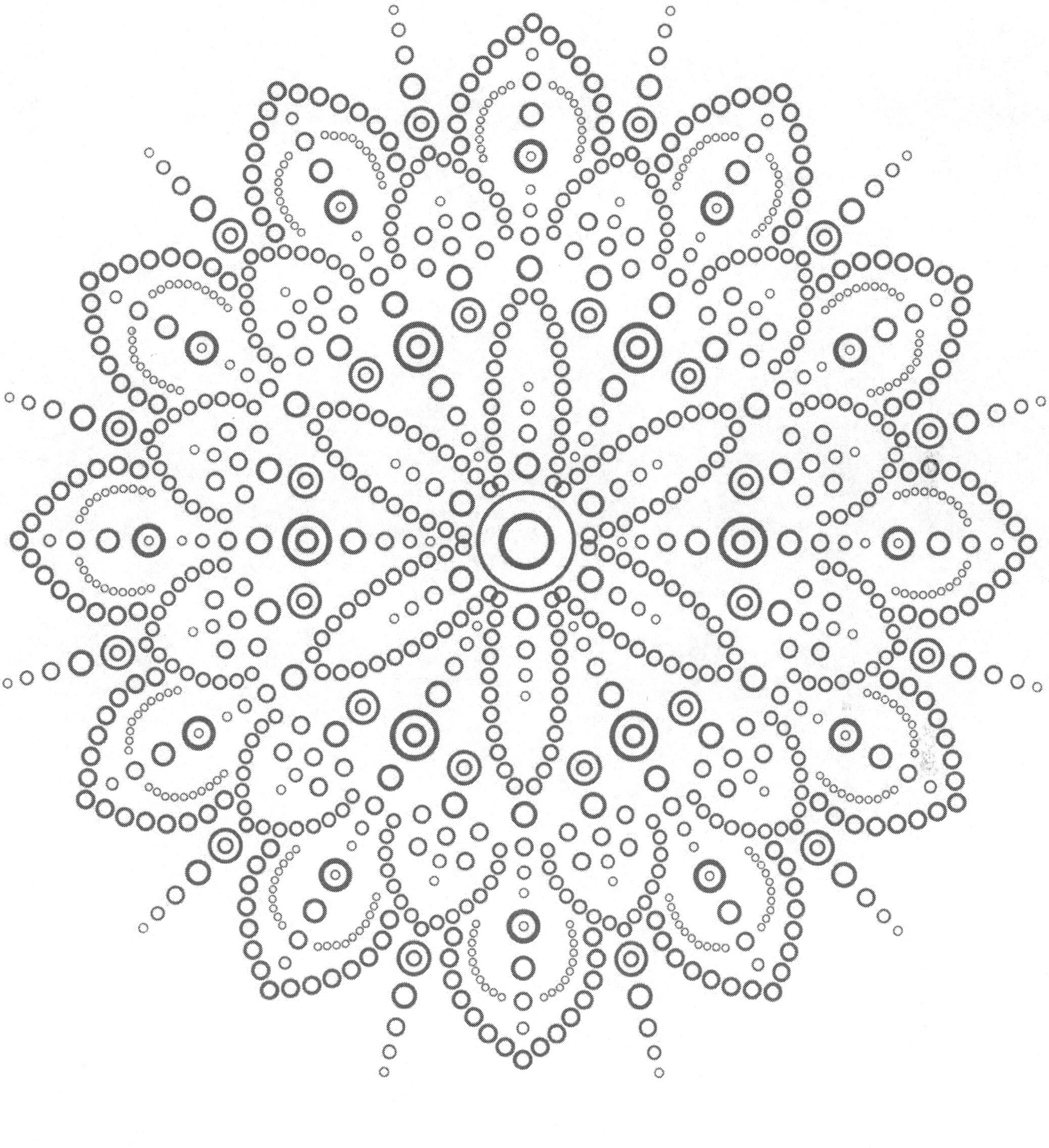

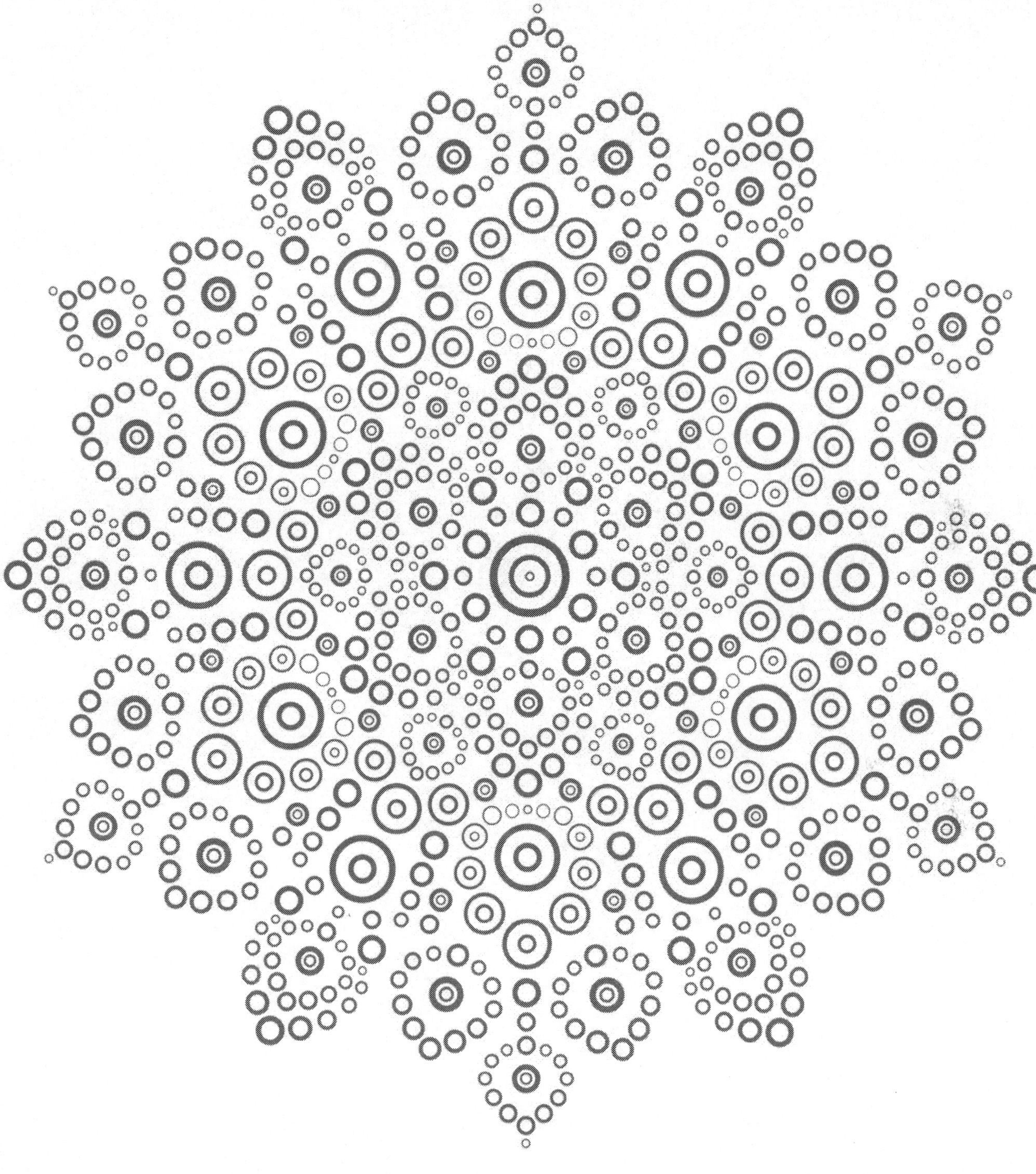

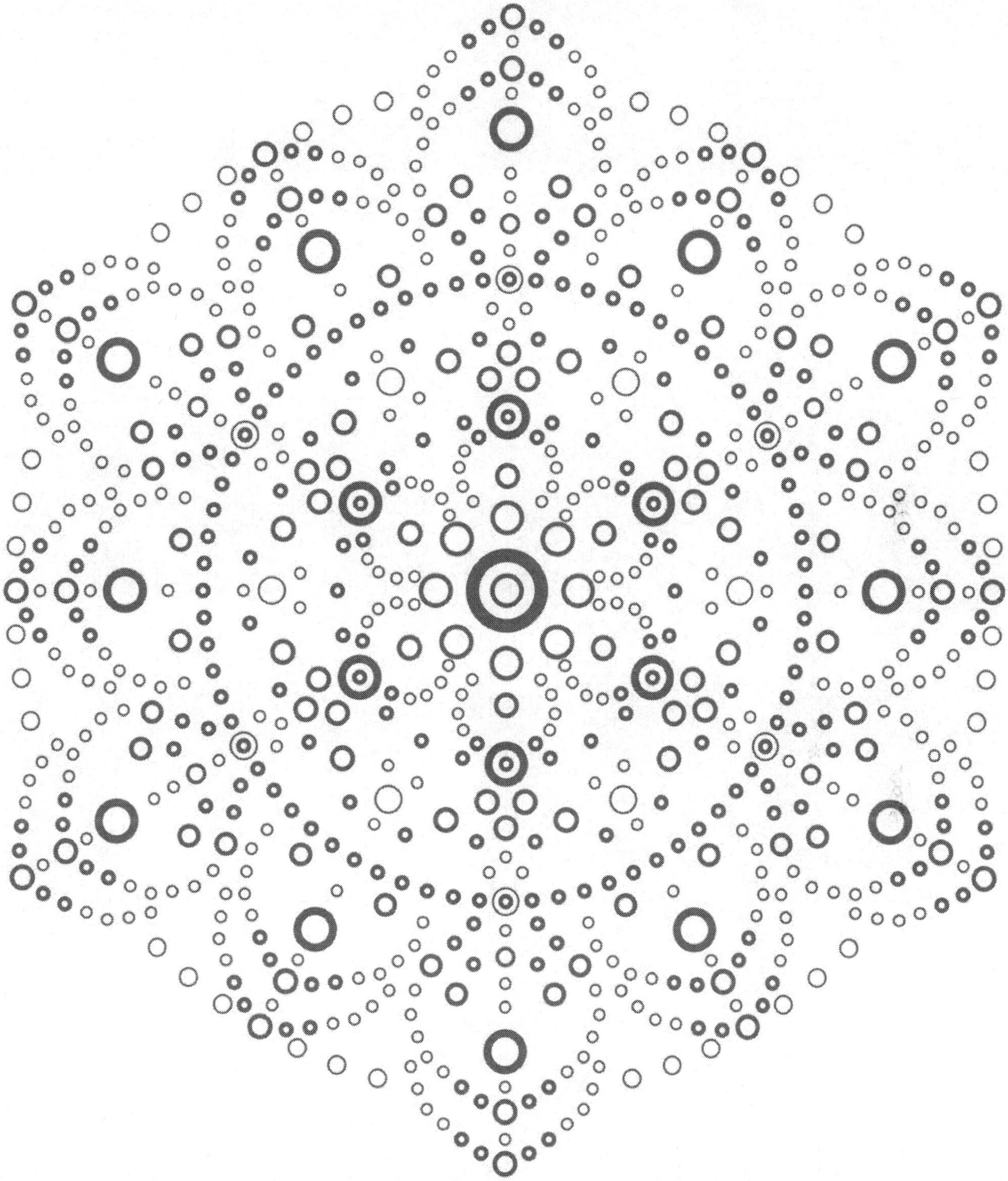

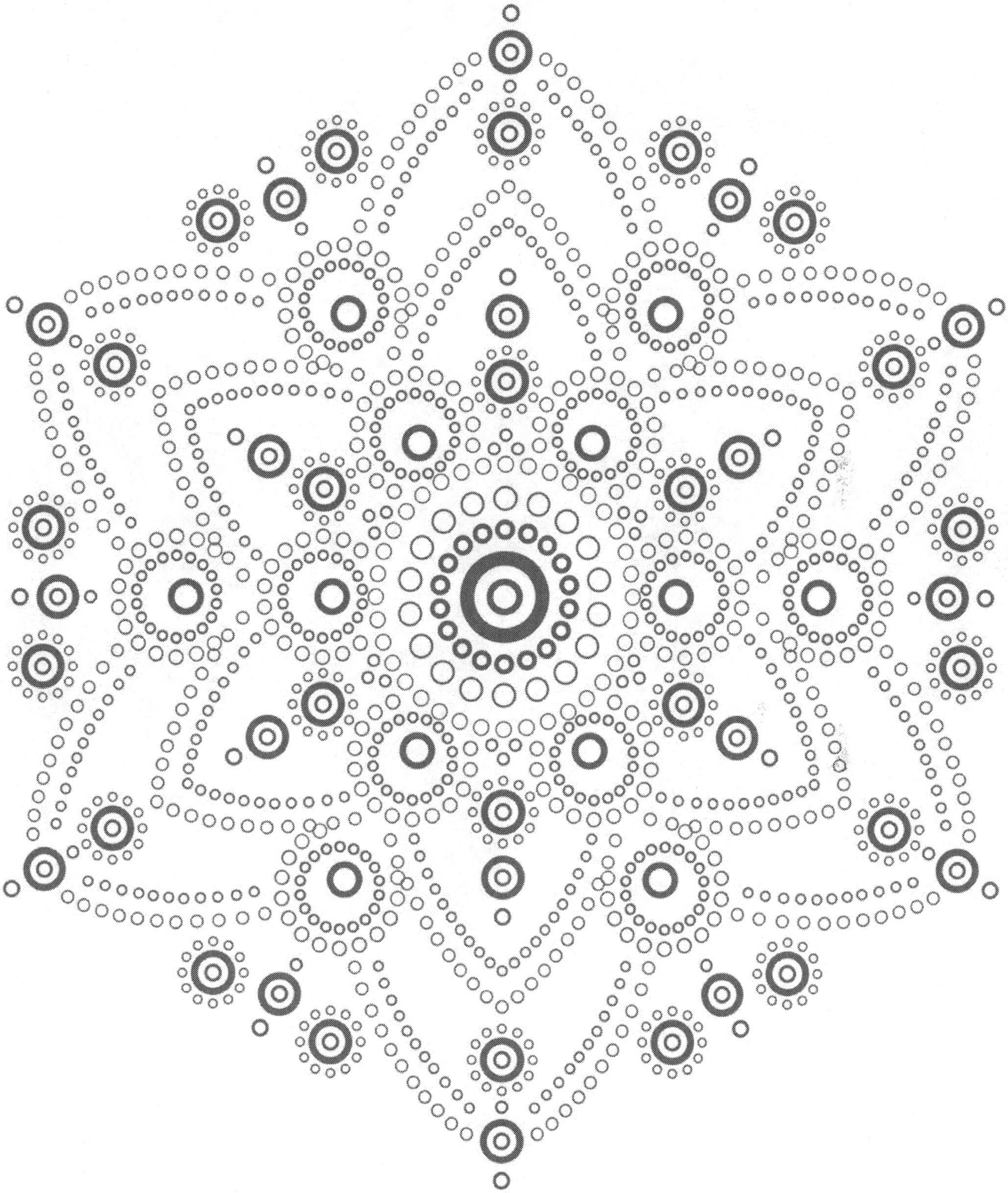

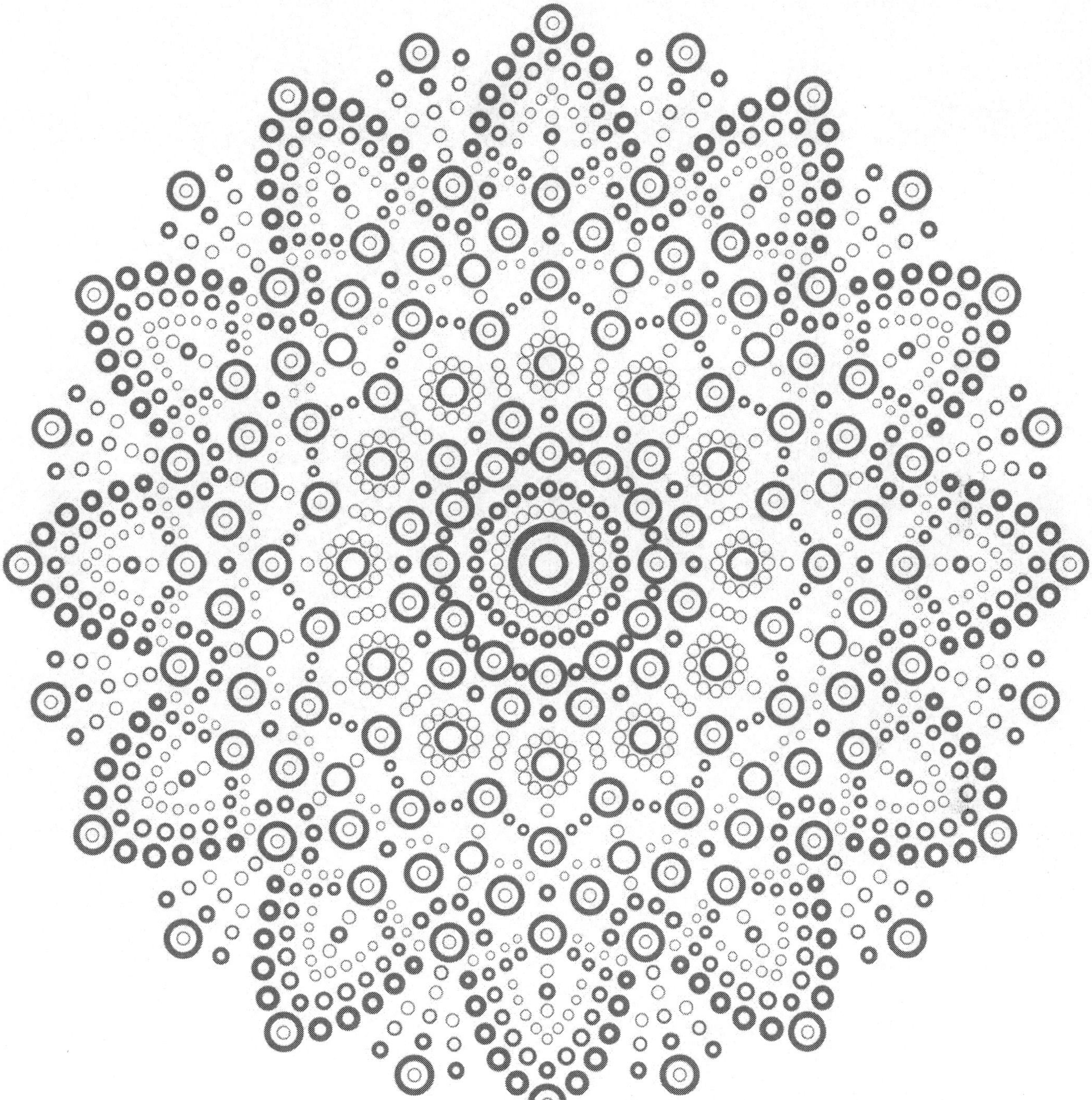

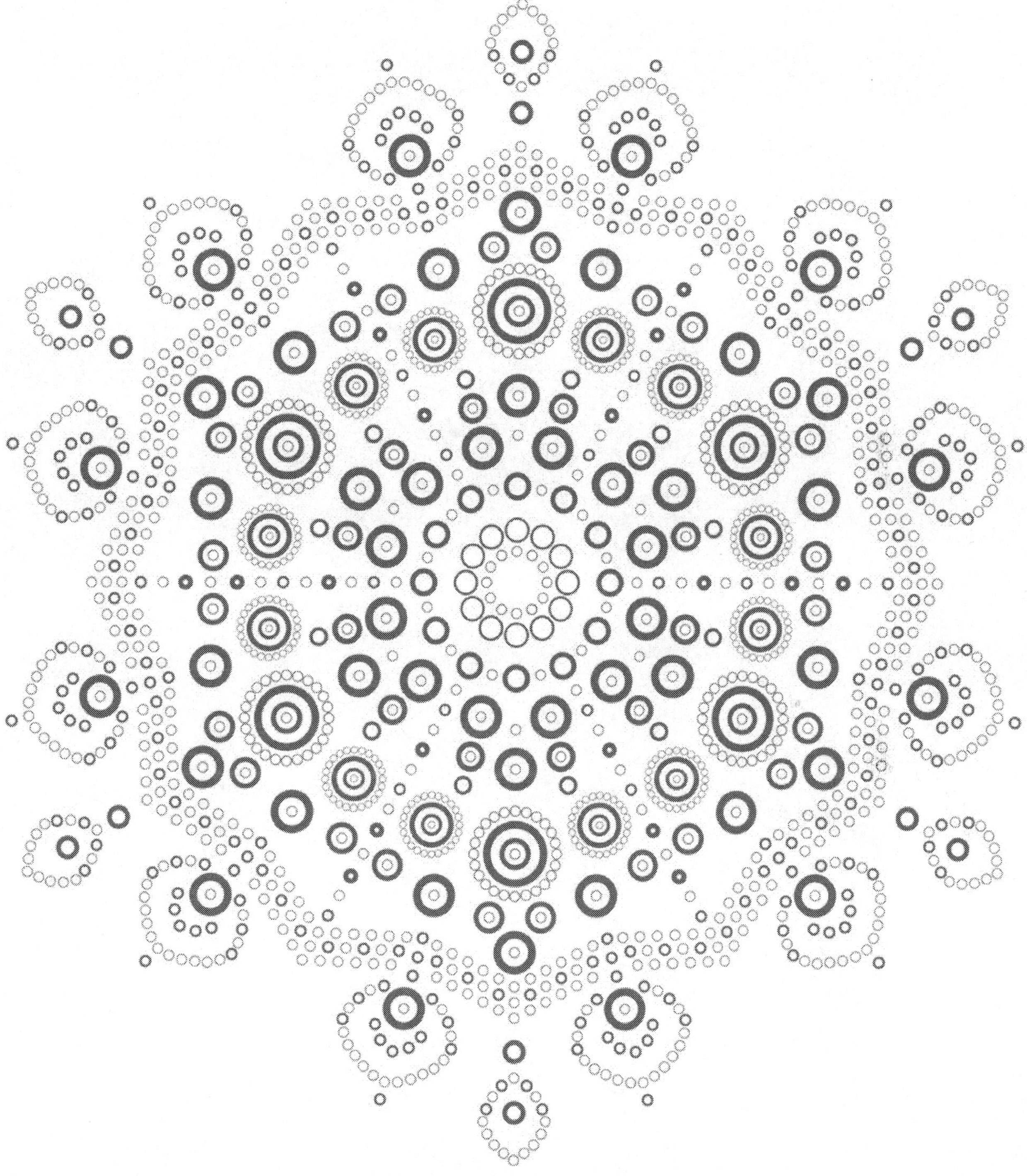

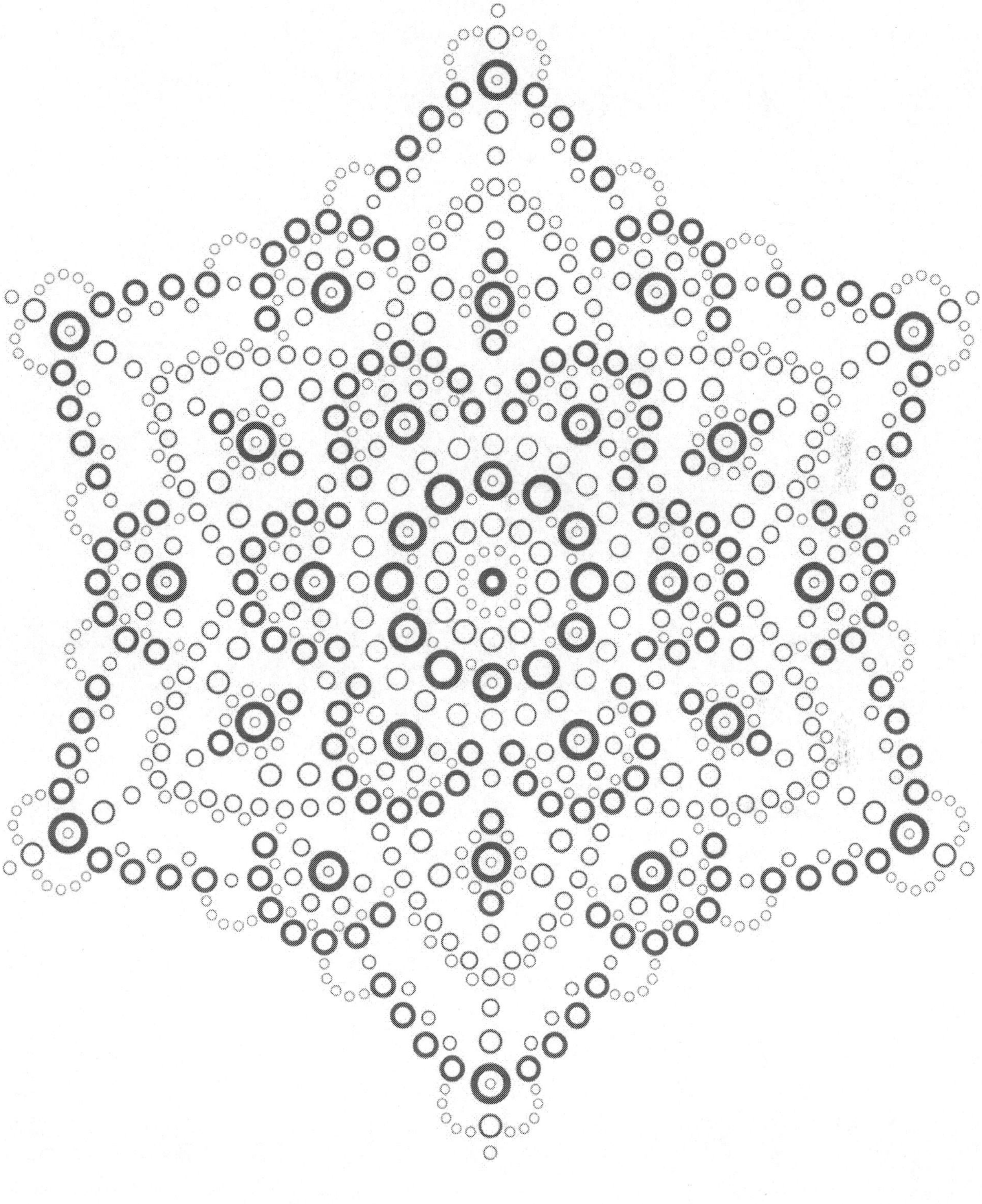

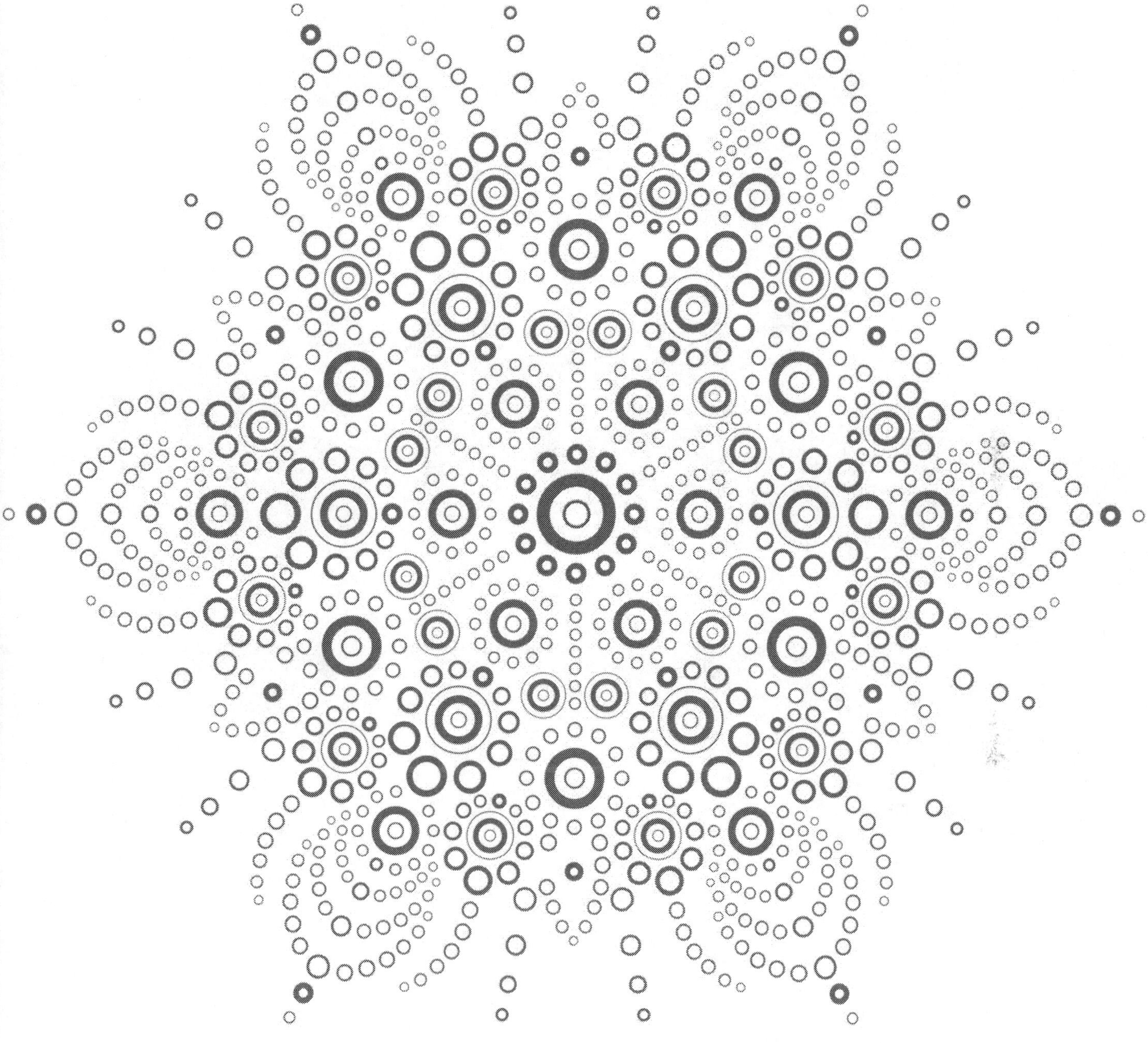

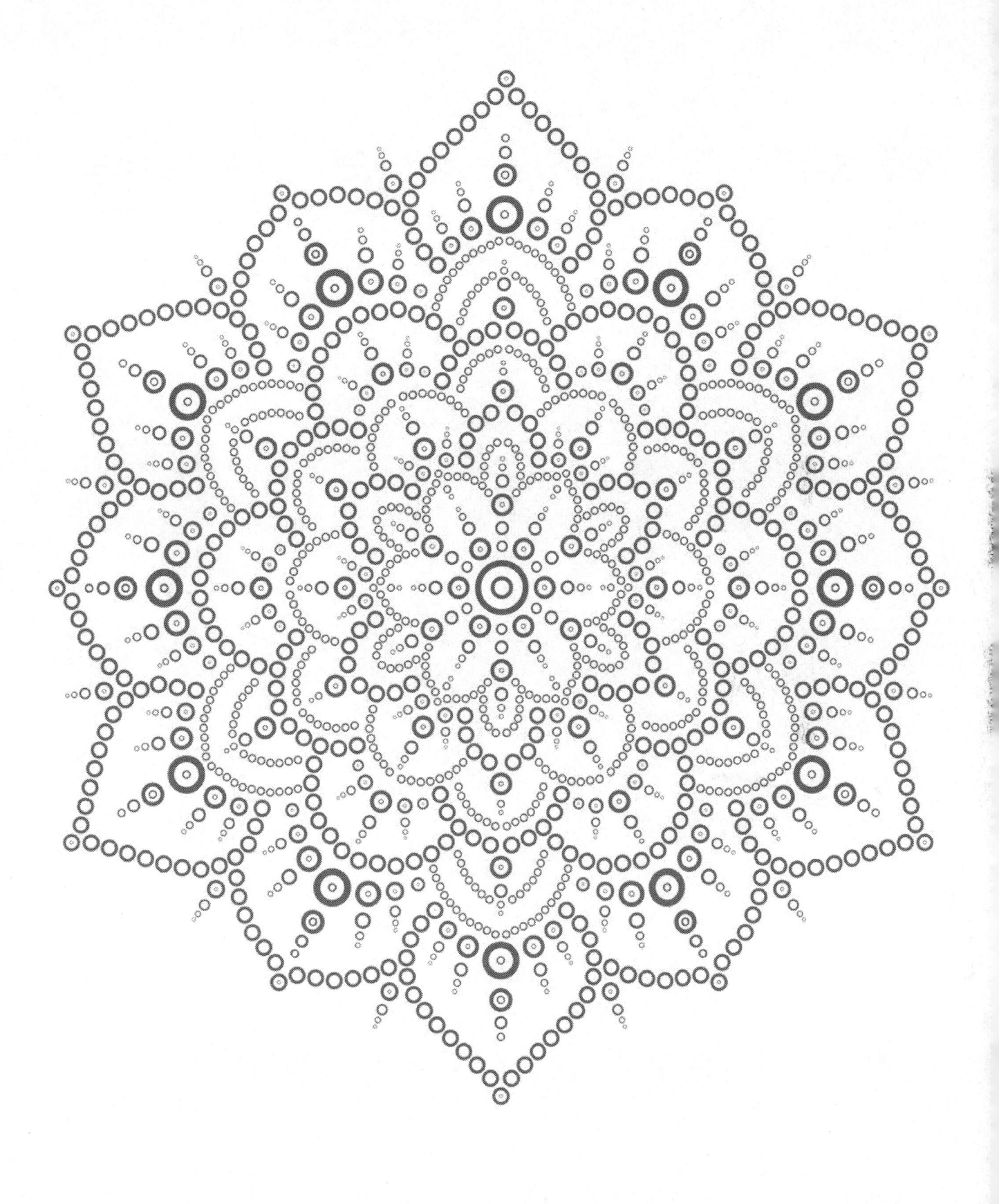

Ende

ICH HOFFE ES HAT DIR GEFALLEN!

Manufactured by Amazon.ca
Bolton, ON